THE BOOK OF

ENGLISH FIREPLACES

A Design for a Chimney Piece.

A 'continued chimneypiece' from *The Gentleman and Cabinet Maker's Director* (1762) by Thomas Chippendale. Rococo at its most extreme.

THE BOOK OF

ENGLISH

FIREPLACES

Alison Kelly

COUNTRY LIFE BOOKS

Published for Country Life Books
by The Hamlyn Publishing Group Ltd.
The Centre, Feltham, Middlesex.

Printed in Great Britain
by Cox & Wyman Ltd.
London, Fakenham and Reading

Contents

List of plates

THE 20TH CENTURY

Foreword

Over the centuries, rooms of any importance in England have been provided with fireplaces, and until within living memory houses would have been uninhabitable without them. It seems surprising therefore that, among the hundreds of books written about every aspect of domestic design, hardly any have been concerned solely with the fireplace and its equipment. We have to go back to 1912 to find a fully illustrated history in L. A. Shuffrey's book *The English Fireplace*. Since then, there have only been a short work by C. G. Rothery, mostly illustrated with fireplaces *ex situ*, and Lawrence Wright's *Home Fires Burning* of 1964, which, like his other domestic investigations, is concerned principally with social history, and only secondarily with taste and fashion in the design of fireplaces.

In the fifty-six years since Shuffrey's book was written, tastes have changed; at that time, architectural historians were not interested in 19th-century design, and indeed a building could not be a historical monument (within the terms of the Act) if it had been begun after the death of Queen Anne. Shuffrey's book reflects this climate of opinion. It covers in very great detail the Elizabethan and Jacobean periods, which he seems particularly to have enjoyed, but becomes slighter in dealing with the 18th century, and leaves the 19th century almost untouched. In this book, I hope to do something to redress the balance.

I have interpreted the word *fireplace* in the widest sense, including the chimneys which are at one end of the flue, as well as the fireplaces at the other. I have also included the hearth equipment, from andirons to grates and stoves, and also the implements for tending the fire. Here there are hideous pitfalls, since grates were changed much more frequently than fireplaces themselves, not from fashion but from necessity. An Adam period grate, for instance, might be changed in the Victorian period for one which burned better; in the 20th century, the anachronistic 19th-century grate might be ripped out again, and a dog-grate restored. Without documentary evidence, it is difficult to be certain whether this grate is an 18th-century one, or a replica made by such a firm as the Carron Iron Company from one of their original Georgian designs. It is unusual to find pieces, such as the grates at Corsham Court, of which both date and manufacturer are known. It must not be assumed that the grates and firedogs shown in this book are necessarily contemporary with the fireplaces in which they stand.

A word should be said about the names of fireside impedimenta. The word *andiron* preceded *firedog*, but by the time of early existing examples, both words were in use. The earliest piece of equipment illustrated (Plate 1) was obviously called something different by its Romano-British owners, but I have called it an andiron for want of any other word. The words *stove* and *grate* seem to have been hopelessly entangled in the late 18th century, a *Bath stove* being to many writers what we call a *hob-grate*. There are also stoves in the sense in which we know the word. *Chimneys*, as mentioned in Chapter I, were in early times taken to refer to the hearth and its surroundings as well as to the flue. There remains the most difficult problem of all, the name of the surround to the fire opening within a room. To most people this is a *fireplace*, and I have, in general, used this word. However, by the 18th century, it was universally referred to as a *chimneypiece*. To avoid switching back and forth from one word to the other, I have generally used the word chimneypiece for 17th to early 19th-century examples. To some people, *chimneypiece* is still correct usage, as against *mantelpiece*, which, though known earlier, does not seem to have come into general usage until the early 19th century. I have avoided the use of the word *mantelpiece*. However, *manteltree* is a very ancient word, meaning the beam forming the lintel of the fire opening, and *mantelshelf* and *overmantel* (to describe an architectural or decorative feature above the fireplace) have been used, since there appear to be no alternatives. The 18th-century phrase *continued chimneypiece*, for fireplace and overmantel together, is now obsolete, unfortunately.

It remains for me to thank those who have helped me in this book; Mr Cyril Staal for information on chimneyboards; Mr John Gloag for introducing me to Isaac Ware's *Complete Body of Architecture*; Mr John Cornforth for information about Chatsworth; Dr Lindsay Boynton for permission to quote from *Furniture History*, Vol. 1, pp. 50–56; Mrs Talbot Rice and the Curator of the Colchester and Essex Museum for having their respective fireplaces specially photographed; the Allied Ironfounders for permission to use their Coalbrookdale catalogue for 1875; the Carron Iron Company for information about their early designs; Messrs Alec Tiranti for permission to use an illustration from Seymour Lindsay's *Iron and Brass Implements of the English House*; Messrs G. Bell and Sons for permission to reproduce an illustration from Raymond Lister's *Decorative Cast Ironwork*; Mr F. M. Mason for information about the Henry VIII andirons at Knole; and the Photographic Library of the Council of Industrial Design for two illustrations from their portfolio of dreadful designs.

Acknowledgements

The chimneypiece in the Queen's Gallery, Hampton Court, Middlesex (Plate 54) is reproduced by gracious permission of Her Majesty the Queen.

The author also wishes to express her gratitude to the following for their help with illustrations:

Albright-Knox Art Gallery, Buffalo: 81; Allied Ironfounders Ltd.: 86, 87, 88, 89; William J. Barrett: 90; Brecht-Einzig Ltd.: 109; Brighton Corporation: 20; S. A. Chandler and Co. Ltd.: 11; Colchester and Essex Museum: 1; Council of Industrial Design: 106; Country Life: 3, 4, 7, 9, 10, 19, 22, 23, 24, 25, 26, 27, 28, 29, 30, 31, 32, 33, 34, 35, 36, 37, 38, 40, 41, 42, 43, 44, 46, 47, 48, 49, 51, 52, 53, 55, 56, 57, 58, 59, 60, 62, 65, 73, 76, 80, 83, 84, 85, 91, 92, 94, 95, 97, 98, 99, 100; Courtauld Institute of Art: 66, 67, 79; Alfred Cracknell, courtesy of Chamberlain, Powell and Son: 110; Gas Council: 102, 103, 108; Hastings Museum: 21 (d); Michael Holford: 13, 17, 18, 21 (a), (b), (c), 61, 63, 69, 72, 73, 75, 77, 101, Frontispiece; House Beautiful: 111; A. F. Kersting: 5, 12; G. P. King: 16; Edward Leigh F.I.B.P., F.R.P.S.: 78; Lady Lever Art Gallery: 68; Minsterstone (Wharf Lane) Ltd.: 107; National Monuments Record: 6, 8, 45, 64, 93; Gwynneth Pennethorne: 70, 71; Radio Times Hulton Picture Library: 96; Royal Commission on Historical Monuments (England): 15; Science Museum: 104; Charles Seely: 2; Marcus W. Taylor: 105; Victoria and Albert Museum: 39, 50, 74, 82; Warburg Institute, University of London: 54; John Webb F.R.P.S.: 14.

1. Early English Fireplaces

'Hearth and Home' has always been a favourite British saying, and for centuries the British have been most contented in front of an open fire; even today, electric fires can be bought with imitation log fires attached. It is interesting therefore that a piece of fireplace equipment for an open hearth goes back almost to the beginnings of British history. It is a double andiron, dug up in Colchester and now exhibited in the Colchester and Essex Museum in Colchester Castle (Plate 1). It is considered to be Romano-British and to date from about 300 AD. It consists of two vertical iron bars, raised on legs and joined together by a cross-piece. The vertical bars (they were later to get the name of *staukes*) rise more than two feet from the ground and then curve over to become animal's heads, with long bull's horns, each finishing in a knob. The andiron stood in the middle of the fire, with the logs propped against it, so that they got plenty of air while burning. A similar piece, with the extra convenience of metal loops to support spits, is illustrated in L. A. Shuffrey's book *The English Fireplace* and is said to be documented in *Archaeologia Cambrensis* (1901) and to have come from Voelas in north Wales. It is also said to be Romano-Celtic. Both these were extremely practical pieces; curiously, they seem to have no surviving descendants apart from the double andiron at Penshurst (Plate 13), which is thought to be no earlier than the 16th century.

As they were built of wood, no domestic Anglo-Saxon buildings have survived. Anglo-Saxon poetry, however, is full of references to the Great Halls where the lords and their retainers lived a communal life, eating, sleeping and amusing themselves together. We can imagine a large barn-like building erected directly on the soil. As the ground floor was quite literally the ground, stamped down, a fire could be lighted at any convenient point. A hearthstone could be used, but it was not essential. Probably the fire would be in the middle of the hall, to allow the maximum number of people to crowd round it. The smoke found its way out through a hole in the roof when the wind was in the right direction. We know that these hearths could be tended with shovels and bellows (this last word being a corruption of the Anglo-Saxon *blaest balg*, the blast-bag) because these words appear by 800 AD in the glossaries used to teach the monks their Latin. We also read that St Dunstan chased the devil all over Sussex with a pair of fire tongs; and though we can disbelieve most of this, the fire tongs were real enough, originally designed for work in a forge, but equally useful for adjusting burning logs.

Equally legendary is the story of King Alfred burning the cakes, but Anglo-Saxon cooking may not have been as primitive as this suggests. The Anglo-Saxon words

1. Romano-British double andiron, found in Colchester. Thought to be 3rd-century AD. Compare the shape of this andiron with the double andiron at Penshurst Place, Plate 13.

2. Fireplace at Colchester Castle, *c.* 1090. The castle was built on the site of a Roman temple, and Roman bricks were used to make the arch of the fire opening, and to line the interior.

Life in the Great Hall continued for centuries in the traditional way. The Norman barons, however, built themselves a new type of accommodation in England after the Conquest. Their castles, at first stockades of wood, developed in the late 11th and 12th centuries into tall, stone keeps or donjons. For safety, the ground floors of these buildings were used for storage of goods or prisoners. This part was inaccessible from outside; the entrance to the castle was at first-floor level, and the Norman baron and his family lived upstairs. The few surviving Norman houses show the same pattern with living accommodation on the upper floor.

This meant that there had to be some new thinking about fireplaces; in the old single-storey hall, the fire could be laid wherever convenient, but fires could hardly be lit in the middle of a wooden, upstairs floor without disastrous results. The hearth had to retreat to the only safe place, the wall. The earliest Norman fireplaces are scooped out of the wall's thickness. Norman castles often had walls many feet thick, from which staircases and even small rooms could be hollowed out,

hlafweard and *hlafdige*, which have come down to us as 'lord' and 'lady,' mean the loaf-guardian and the loaf-giver – the man who saw that there was a supply of bread, and the woman who had it distributed fairly. This implies that some sort of baking must have been done. The Bayeux Tapestry, which is now believed to have been embroidered in Britain, portrays a scene where quite elaborate preparations for a meal are taking place. A cooking pot stands on an iron rack over a fire which is contained in a firebasket on legs. The meat is threaded on to skewers. There is also something which appears to be a free-standing oven, from which a cook is removing little loaves on to a tray, using tongs so as not to burn his fingers. The women who embroidered the tapestry no doubt copied familiar scenes, so that we can assume that, by the second half of the 11th century, efficient and varied cooking apparatus was available, at any rate for the noble household.

3. Fireplace in the upper hall of the Norman keep at Castle Hedingham, Essex, *c.* 1140. The hearth is semicircular. The brickwork below the fireplace is much later.

so that there was plenty of space for the fire.

The earliest wall fireplaces surviving seem to be those at Colchester Castle (Plate 2), dating from about 1090. The castle was built on the site of a Roman temple, and Roman brick was available for building. The fireplaces have roughly arched openings, with Roman bricks used on their edges to make the voussoirs shaping the arch. The hearth is also roughly semicircular, and the wall inside is a curve of Roman brick set in herring-bone pattern. There is no proper chimney; a funnel of brickwork slopes towards the outside of the wall, dividing about eight feet up, into two smaller funnels which reach the outside on either side of the buttress. In theory, one or the other of the funnels could be closed with a shutter, so that the smoke went out on whichever side of the buttress happened to be the lee-side at the time. In practice, at least one of the fireplaces was on the western side of the castle, so that its buttress, in the normal English conditions of prevailing westerly winds, did not have a lee-side. Rain drips in today, and no doubt came in copiously when the fireplace was in use. Abourt forty years later, and much more sophisticated, are the wall fireplaces at Castle Hedingham, Essex (Plate 3). Here also there are arched openings, more elaborate on the upper than the lower floor. Both have chevron ornament, with a double row on the upper fireplace, and attached columns with cushion capitals at each side, so that the fireplace opening is like a low, Norman church archway. All this is neatly carved in pinkish stone. Inside, the fireplaces are roughly built of ragstone, and are more beehive-shaped than those at Colchester, with a much smaller opening to what could almost be called the chimney. This flue also recedes at a steeper angle, so that daylight cannot be seen when one is standing inside the fireplace; it may well have been more effective than the Colchester design for keeping out the weather. Fireplaces similar to those at Castle Hedingham can be seen at Rochester Castle, and belong to the same period. As Rochester has lost its floors, it is not possible to examine the hearths and flues properly.

Later in the 12th century, attempts were

4. Michelham Priory, Sussex. 13th-century fireplace with large hood tapering and sloping back to the wall. The small bracket at the side is to hold a candle. Tudor fireback.

made to direct the smoke up something resembling a chimney. At Porchester Castle there is an internal chimney about ten feet high, ending in a little vault; slits in the outside wall, just below this level, were intended to draw the smoke away. Other chimneys were simply shafts attached to the exterior wall just above the level of the fireplace. These could have open tops, but more usually had a stone cone-shaped roof, with slits below to let out the smoke (Plate 8). That a chimney draws better if it reaches above the level of the roof does not seem to have been discovered for some time.

By the beginning of the 13th century, the fire had edged a little way in front of the wall and rested on a hearthstone built into the floor. A great stone canopy above it directed the smoke upwards and backwards towards the outer wall. Often in early examples this hood is pyramidal in shape. It could be made of stone, as all the surviving examples are, but was often of wood or plaster. The remains of one which had a stone framework, but a wood or plaster hood, was discovered at

5. Abingdon Abbey, Berkshire. Chimney of the building called The Chequer, 13th-century. Dr Nikolaus Pevsner considers this to be the most interesting chimney of its date in England. It has a roof with four gables, and the smoke comes out through the lancet-shaped slits in each gable.

Pride Hill, Shrewsbury, in 1957. The canopy could be held up at the sides by a column or cluster of columns (as at Conisburgh Castle), but a more convenient arrangement, in that it allowed more space at ground level for people to cluster round the fire, was to have the canopy supported on stone corbels or brackets. It was difficult to find blocks of stone long enough to span from corbel to corbel, and so the lintel was often built up of stones ingeniously *joggled*—that is, cut with angular outlines on their sides to key into each other. The fireplace canopy at Boothby Pagnall Manor House, dating from the very beginning of the 13th century, is of this kind. A small angle bracket, often to be seen at each side of the fireplace, in the angle between the canopy and the wall, served two useful purposes. It made a lateral support for the canopy, and it also provided a useful shelf on which to stand a candle or rushlight.

These canopied fireplaces were in fashion throughout the 13th century in upper rooms of castles and houses, and the taste continued into the 14th century, growing in elegance and refinement. However, by the 15th century they had gone out of fashion in Britain, though visitors to Italy or France will have seen examples there of much later dates. Before the taste for them disappeared, some splendid examples had been built, such as Prior Crauden's fireplace at Ely, of about 1325, which has corbels of a double scrolled pattern, and a battlemented border all the way round. Meare Manor House, of about the same date, has a simpler but well-proportioned hood, which, instead of being flat, comes to a slight angle down the middle. Michelham Priory, Sussex, has a flat pyramidal hood (Plate 4). The dignity of these designs prompts the

6. The Abbot's Kitchen, Glastonbury Abbey, mid-14th-century. The four fireplaces were set diagonally across the corners of the square lower part of the building; their flues led directly upwards into the open air. Smoke and fumes from the central part of the kitchen came out through the octagonal lantern.

7. Penshurst Place, Kent. Central hearth of brick. The logs are propped against a double andiron of wrought iron, which is either the original one, or an early replacement. There was a *louver* in the roof to take away the smoke; this has now been covered over. Mid-14th-century hall; andiron believed to be 16th-century.

question as to why the English abandoned this type of fireplace so soon, while other countries continued to be satisfied with it.

Even where there was a projecting hood, part of the fireplace was behind the wall line, scooped into the thickness of the wall. By the 15th century, in most places, this excavation became much deeper, so that the whole fire could be accommodated behind the wall line. The canopy could shrink to a projection of a foot or less, like the rudimentary hood at Red Lion House, Burford, or could disappear altogether, leaving a rectangular opening, or a Tudor arch. Several late 15th-century fireplaces have handsome decoration above the lintel. Some have large quatrefoils in a row

8. Kitchen chimney at Manor Farm, Preston Plucknett, Somerset. First half of the 15th century. The chimney has a solid cap, and the smoke came out through the small Gothic windows at the sides. The farm was originally the grange of the abbey of Bermondsey.

gives the latest particulars of castle-building in the 1340s, mentions 'a cheyer before the chemne ther charcoale brenned'—the word here clearly means a fireplace. The *chemne* could also mean the fireplace and flue together, or it could mean the chimney in its modern sense, the flue projecting through the roof. *Sir Gawaine* mentions 'chalk wyte chimnees' on the roof of the castle; chalk-white sounds surprising, but a number of plastered chimneys had unexpectedly long lives. Nathaniel Lloyd knew of one surviving until this century; and the London ordnances of the 14th century decreed that chimneys were to be no longer of wood, but of stone, tiles or plaster. With the multiplication of small rooms, each with its fireplace, chimney-stacks made up of multiple flues came into use. Harlech Castle, of the 1280s, has a quadruple stack, and these later became common. With the increased use of brick, chimney flues in brickwork would be built from ground level, serving fireplaces on several floors; they can often be seen projecting from the walls of wood-frame houses (Plate 9). Chimneys were at first usually round, and later polygonal, with solid caps and vents near the top of the shaft.

Meanwhile, the Great Hall, the large ground-floor room open to the rafters, and still considered to be the centre of the house, continued much as before. The central fireplace remained until astonishingly late dates. The Great Hall at Penshurst Place (Plate 7), of the 1340s, has retained its central hearth, with an octagonal brick area instead of a hearthstone, and central hearths were remembered, and regretted in some cases, as late as the reign of Elizabeth I. William Harrison, in his *Description of England*, published in the 1580s, thought that his forbears had been protected from many diseases by being well kippered in wood smoke. 'Now have we manie chimnies, and yet our tenderlings complaine of rheumes, catarhs and poses ... For as the smoke in those daies was supposed to be a sufficient hardning for the timber of the house, so it was reputed a far better medicine to keepe the goodman and his familie from the quack or pose, wherewith as then verie few were oft acquainted.'

(Plate 12); examples can be found at Burford, Salisbury and Axmouth. A few—two of them in Exeter, in the Deanery Hall and in Exeter Palace (Plate 11) surviving to demonstrate the splendour of great clerics' houses—have elaborate heraldic carving. Heraldry also appears on the fireplaces at Tattershall Castle (Plate 10). These fireplaces were in the smaller, private (often upstairs) rooms in which the nobility now passed most of their time, leaving the Great Hall to their retainers except for formal dining and entertainments. Such fireplaces had, by the 14th century, developed adequate chimneys; the dating of these presents problems, as the word 'chimney' was used in several different meanings. *Sir Gawaine and the Grene Knight*, a poem which

9. Rufford Old Hall, Lancashire. Stone chimney attached to a timber-framed hall of the late 15th century, serving the fireplace in the wall. The lantern in the roof replaces an original *louver*, serving a central hearth.

Chaucer, describing the house of his 'povre widwe', said that 'ful sooty was hir bour and eek [also] hir halle'; and most Great Halls must have been much the same. Originally, the smoke from the central hearth must have made its way out through a hole in the roof; as this let the rain in always, while it only let the smoke out when the wind was in the right direction, a more convenient device was evolved, the *louver* (or *luver, lover, lewer, luuer, louvre* or any other variation of spelling which appealed to the medieval writer). The word is said to come from the French *ouvert*, or *l'ouvert*. This was turret-shaped, with openings in the sides and a solid top. Sometimes, the openings had little gables over them to throw off the wet, sometimes the sides had wood or stone sloping slats like a venetian blind. Occasionally, pottery *louvers* have been found. A most attractive example, green-glazed and shaped like a pagoda, was discovered in Nottingham as recently as 1961.

10. Tattershall Castle, Lincolnshire. A fireplace in the keep, begun in 1435. The four-centred Tudor arch has a band of shields carved above and crenellations at the top. In the brickwork above is a relieving arch, and there is herring-bone brickwork inside the fireplace. The hearth is raised a few inches above the floor.

11. Fireplace from the Bishop's Palace, Exeter, late 15th-century. Heraldic decoration includes the royal arms at the top, as well as the arms of the bishop and the diocese. Fireplace interior reduced in modern times.

Margaret Wood, in her definitive book, *The English Mediaeval House*, dates it at about 1300.

Very decorative *louvers* were evolved: the beautiful spiry turret on Westminster Hall, though a replacement, is supposed to follow the original design. Middle Temple Hall, of Elizabethan date, was built with a *louvred* roof, and Trinity College Hall, at Cambridge, was built with a three-tiered *louver* as late as 1605. The inconvenient arrangement persisted even when difficulties had to be overcome to

12. The Abbot's Parlour, Muchelney Abbey, fireplace *c.* 1508. Splendidly carved design of quatrefoils, leaves and fruit, making one of the finest pre-Reformation fireplaces in the country. The lions at the top are rather oddly placed. It has been suggested that they were originally somewhere else, or they could perhaps have ornamented the top of a painted panel above the fireplace.

13. Double andiron at Penshurst Place drawn without logs so that the construction can be seen. Compare with Plate 1.

install a central hearth. The Great Hall at Hampton Court, dating from the time of Henry VIII, is raised on a high undercroft. It has, nevertheless, a central hearthstone, which has to be supported from below by a large brick pier with corbels.

Margaret Wood thinks that many of these central hearths had canopies over them to direct the smoke up to the *louver*, and has found traces of such canopies in three Yorkshire houses. These would have improved conditions in the average Great Hall; they must, all the same, have often been very uncomfortable, and sometimes dangerous. As a 15th-century writer cautiously remarked, 'When smoke medled with fyre cometh out of an house by the louerys, men . . . will saye that the house shall go on fyre'.

A part of the house which was expected to go on fire, and so was often built separately, was the kitchen. However, a few stone kitchens have survived to show us what cooking hearths must have been like in medieval times. A particularly fine one has survived from the 14th century at Glastonbury, and belonged to the abbot's quarters (Plate 6). This kitchen shows considerable ingenuity in planning; the building outside is square, but inside it is an octagon, with four fireplaces cutting across the outer corners. An octagonal roof rises to a lantern, with another smaller lantern on top, thus providing a funnel to dispose of heat and fumes from the central part of the kitchen, while each cooking fire has its own triangular hearth and individual tapering flue above. Durham also has an

octagonal kitchen with a beautifully vaulted roof and a *lantern-louver;* and there is another, secular, octagonal kitchen at Berkeley Castle. Kitchens, with their open fires, were unavoidably very hot–Chaucer's cook had a 'fyre-reed cherubinnes face' from his occupation–and it is interesting to know that steps were taken at such an early date to improve working conditions.

At the beginning of this chapter, we discussed the Romano-British andiron at Colchester Museum. It must have been the ancestor of many similar pieces, but curiously, the word 'andiron' does not appear in manuscripts before the 14th century. The first mention known to the Oxford Dictionary is of 1314, and refers to an 'aundiron'. This is a corruption of Old French *andier;* educated people in England still spoke French, but, as Chaucer pointed out, it was often 'Frenche of Stratford atte Bowe', and by association with the iron of which it was made, the word 'andiron' developed. 'Firedog' seems to have been a later alternative for much the same thing, though by Elizabethan times a distinction seems to have been made between large andirons to support spits, dog-irons or firedogs to hold up the logs, and creepers, which were little stands to raise the smaller bits of wood. The shape of a firedog does vaguely suggest the diagrammatic outline of a dog, with two front legs, a vertical piece in the front called the *stauke* with a knob at the top suggesting the neck and head, and a long bar going back horizontally and suggesting the body. This bar was called the *billet-bar*, as logs were called *billets*. As we have seen, the Romano-British smith saw his double andiron in animal form. Usually a pair of andirons would be set one on each side of the hearth. The double andiron, of Colchester type, with the two andirons joined by a bar, seems only to have survived on the central hearth in the hall at Penshurst Place (Plate 13). The very plain specimen there is thought to date from the 16th century. Such a sensible piece of equipment seems likely to have been made at other times between 300 and 1500 AD, and it seems probable that many other pieces of similar type have been destroyed. Some may in fact survive, their purpose unrecognised.

2. The Tudor and Jacobean Periods

Once the great overhanging hood above the hearth had gone out of fashion, the fireplace could, if necessary, be quite plain. All that was needed was a fire opening in the wall, and a hearth which communicated with a chimney. The opening could be rectangular, and was usually this shape as a matter of convenience when the house was made of wood, and the lintel of the chimney opening was one great beam. If the house was of stone or the newly fashionable brick, a flattened Tudor arch was often preferred. Plenty of draught was needed to get a good fire going, and this meant that the hearth and the base of the chimney were both wide and deep. At times, this area was so large that people could squeeze inside the opening and bake them-selves beside the fire. A brick and stone chimneypiece in the Victoria and Albert Museum, London, has a little stone seat built into one side, and benches or settles could also be put in. The Elizabethan Sir Philip Sidney, remarking that the power of poetry was so great that it could draw old men from the chimney corner, was probably thinking of this hot and draught-free refuge for old, cold bones. Ovens were built into the walls on each side of the fireplace. To make the best use of the heat, they were usually narrow and very deep from back to front, sometimes stretching the whole depth of the fireplace. Special flat shovels, called *peles*, were needed to retrieve loaves set to bake at the back of the oven. Considering their usefulness, and the fact that

14. *Interior of a kitchen at Newcastle, South Wales* by Thomas Rowlandson. The aquatint was reproduced in H. Wigstead's *Remarks on a Tour to North and South Wales in the Year* 1797 published by W. Wigstead in 1800. The caption reads 'A pleasant village; at a decent Inn here, a dog is employed as a turnspit; great care is taken that this animal does not observe the cook approach the larder; if he does, he immediately hides himself for the remainder of the day, and the guest must be contented with more humble fare than intended.'

15. Hampton Court Palace. Henry VIII's kitchen, 1529–40. The right-hand fireplace has iron spit-supports built into the brickwork partitions which divide it into three sections.

everybody ate bread, it is surprising that ovens were not more widespread than they seem to have been. As late as the 18th century, people made pies at home, and sent them to the baker to be cooked. Dr Johnson (not, of course, a model housekeeper) sent his baking out as late as the 1780s.

Otherwise, the equipment of the kitchen fireplace remained as before. We have seen that meat was roasted on spits from Norman times if not earlier, and in the course of time various methods were devised to keep the spit turning, so that the food cooked evenly. The first turnspit, who did it manually, was a kitchen assistant (we remember the luckless pretender Lambert Simnel) but by the second half of the 16th century there were clockwork or draught-operated spit-jacks to do this repetitive job. There were also firedogs (live, not metal) who were trained to run round and round. Dr Caius, of Gonville and Caius College, Cambridge, mentioned that there was a special breed of dog for this purpose. Such dogs, considering the ease with which a clockwork spit could be made, survived to astonishingly late dates. Thomas Rowlandson, at the beginning of the 19th century, drew a farmhouse kitchen with a small dog shut up in a wheel-shaped cage, turning the roasting spit (Plate 14).

Cardinal Wolsey's kitchen at Christ Church College, Oxford, still in daily use, illustrates vividly the size and scale of the Tudor kitchen. The Hampton Court kitchen (Plate 15) is similar. Even when as high as this – the Wolsey kitchen is a cube the height of three storeys – it was extremely hot, as almost all cooking was done over the open fire. As John Earle, in 1628, rather unfeelingly said of the cook, 'The kitchen is his hell and he the devil in it, where he and his meat fry together'.

The smith had to make equipment, not only for the kitchen, but for all the rooms in the house. Metal firedogs became grander and more decorative. Andirons with brass knobs on them became a commonplace in Elizabethan inventories, and sometimes they sprout great rosettes and scrolls of silver, which must have sparkled gaily in the firelight. A very fine pair of andirons, now at Knole, in Kent (Plate 16), are among the very few which can be dated accurately, since they bear the arms of Henry VIII and Anne Boleyn, and must have been made during the three years 1533–36, during which Queen Anne managed to retain her crown – and her head. Hever, Anne's home, is a few miles away, and the andirons came from there. It was during the reign of Henry VIII that well-educated Englishmen first heard of what was happening in the arts in Renaissance Italy. In compliment to the new style, which strove to emulate the art of classical antiquity, the well-informed householder might have the *staukes* of his andirons cast in the form of classical columns – or as near as the smith could get to them (Plates 17, 18, 19).

Two pieces of smith's work have so far not been mentioned. The curfew was the signal, from Norman days, that householders must make sure that their fires were safe for the night. The word is derived from the French *couvre-feu* and people were able literally to cover the remains of their fires with a metal shield looking something like half a Victorian dishcover (Plate 20). A copper specimen is in the Brighton Museum, and several more (though Dutch rather than English) are in the Victoria and Albert Museum, London.

16. Firedogs decorated with the arms of Henry VIII and Anne Boleyn. They were made between 1533 and 1536, the years of Anne's reign, for Hever Castle, Anne's home. They were bought for Knole, Sevenoaks, about ten miles from Hever, about 150 years ago, and are still in the house.

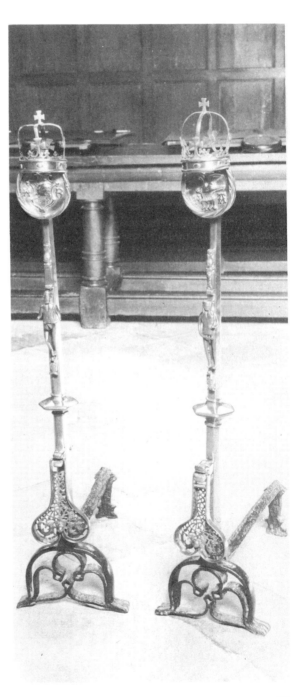

17. Three cast iron andirons, the *staukes* in the form of classical columns, one dated 1677. Victoria and Albert Museum.

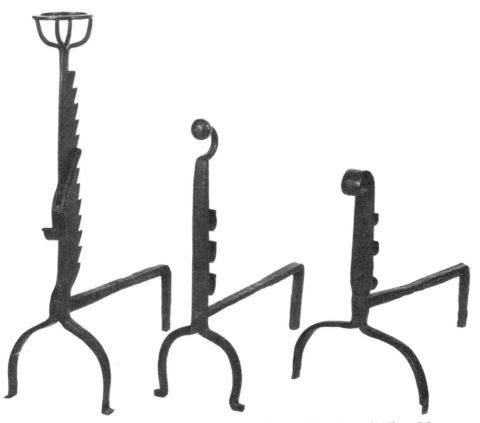

18. Three wrought iron andirons. Victoria and Albert Museum.

19. Elizabethan cast iron fireback dated 1565 and with the initials E.R. The cast iron firedogs, also initialled E.R., are decorated with the English craftsman's version of classical terms who wear Ionic capitals on their heads. From Ockwells Manor, Berkshire.

Another safety device was the fireback. To prevent the back wall of the fireplace from getting too hot, it became customary to place an iron plate against it. These plates were made in Britain from the time when the method of casting iron was first understood, but there is some controversy as to whether this was in the 14th or 15th century. Specimens are known from the 15th century, but as the heyday of the elaborately decorated fireback was in the 16th and 17th centuries, it seems more appropriate to mention them here.

Sand moulds were used and raised patterns were produced by pressing pieces of carved wood into the sand. A very early example has a decoration crudely made by pressing bits of

20. Curfew made of repoussé brass. Late 17th-century. Brighton Museum.

a.

b.

21. *(a)* Cast iron Sussex fireback dated 1649 showing the emblems of France, Scotland, and England. Victoria and Albert Museum.
    (b) Cast iron fireback with the royal arms and the badges of the Tudor sovereigns. 16th-century. Victoria and Albert Museum.
    (c) Cast iron Sussex fireback showing andirons bearing a shield with the initials H.N. and two staples interlaced. 16th-century. Victoria and Albert Museum.
    (d) 17th-century cast iron Sussex fireback, inscribed 'Richard Lenard Founder at Bred Fournis'. The bearded smith is shown with his tools, wheelbarrow and dog, and in the bottom right-hand corner, a fireback inscribed R.L. Hastings Museum.

c.

rope into the sand. The molten iron ran into depressions in the mould and the result was a plate of iron with a bas-relief on it. Early firebacks were of a horizontal oblong shape, to fit the wide fireplaces then in use; as time went on, and the fireplaces became smaller, the fireback became a vertical oblong, often with an arched top. Patterns were delightfully varied (Plate 21). It was not difficult to make a new design, and customers could order their coat of arms, figures, animals, or anything else that appealed to them. One gruesome fireback has a design showing Richard Woodman and his wife being burnt at the stake during the religious persecutions of Queen Mary Tudor. The horribly literal imagination of its owner must have got satisfaction from consigning this unhappy pair again and again to the flames, each time he lit his fire. A more agreeable design shows the Brede smith, with the tools of his trade (Plate 21). It is dated 1636, and has the inscription 'Richard Lenard Founder at Bred Fournis'. It has not travelled far during its life and is now in Hastings Museum, eight miles away. There are andirons to match, incorporating little figures, which are thought to represent Richard, on the *staukes*. The region around Brede, on the Sussex-Kent border, was the great iron-

d.

working district of the country in the Tudor period. The iron was smelted with charcoal from the abundant oak woods of the Weald, and many of the finest firebacks extant come from this area. The shortage of oak wood, combined with the discovery that iron could be better smelted with coal, eventually killed the Sussex trade, but the Ordnance Survey map still shows traces of it in the 'Furnace Farms', 'Hammer Ponds', 'Forge Cottages' and 'Foundry Woods' which still abound as place names. A particularly fine collection of firebacks can be seen a little further west, at Petworth House, where the National Trust have enlivened the kitchen passages with a series of some forty or fifty firebacks, of all dates and styles.

Early Tudor fireplaces are similar to late medieval ones. The same flat arches, heraldic decorations and late Perpendicular details appear on both. Often there is no decoration at all beyond a neatly carved moulding round the fire opening (Plate 22). Wolsey's fireplaces, in the part of Hampton Court built by him, are in this style. Ceiling and frieze in 'Wolsey's Lodging' are splendidly painted and gilded, but the fireplace is unobtrusive and utilitarian. Since Wolsey loved everything about him to be handsome, and spent vast sums on his household equipment, it must be assumed that during the 1520s and 1530s the fireplace was not considered to be an important feature in the decoration of a room.

All this changed as Renaissance ideas began to filter into this country. They came late, of course, to England, and often in a garbled form. Few people had had the opportunity of travelling to Italy and looking at complete buildings in the new style. Most of them had to rely on the illustrations of details – a sculptured figure, a column, a section of an entablature – which were available in books, and they thought that such ornaments could be put on traditional houses as icing is put on a cake. This often resulted in strange proportions, and still stranger combinations of classical, traditional and heraldic detail. This became more noticeable as a new interest in the fireplace developed. It became the focal point of the whole decorative scheme of a room (Plate 23); the chimneypiece itself, with its decoration,

22. Sawston Hall, Cambridge. Fireplace *c.* 1560. The Tudor four-centred arch still remains, while the overmantel is decorated with very restrained classical detail. Early type of cast iron fireback and 16th or 17th-century andirons. The fireplace has been little altered, although it has clearly smoked a good deal. Fender modern.

23. Burghley House, Northamptonshire. Fireplace in the Great Hall, *c.* 1560. Early use of classical motifs by themselves, without Gothic additions, and a surprisingly austere design for the date. Grate and fireplace interior Victorian.

24. Reigate Priory, Surrey. The stone fireplace, *c.* 1540, has the arms of the Howard family, while the woodwork surround has the royal arms and Tudor roses and so must have come from some royal house. Grate 19th or 20th-century. Andirons of 16th-century type.

might be seven or eight feet wide, and with the overmantel the whole construction might stretch from floor to ceiling.

A good example of this change of taste, indeed an example where we can see the change actually taking place, is the fireplace at Reigate Priory (Plate 24). Originally there was a fairly modest stone chimneypiece, with a frieze of nude figures, jester, and so on, which suggest that a few Renaissance ideas had filtered in. Dr Nikolaus Pevsner dates it at about 1540. A little later, possibly in about 1550, this relatively simple fireplace was surrounded by a vast carved wood chimneypiece and overmantel crammed with a mixture of Renaissance and traditional ornament. The

royal arms are set in strapwork decoration, and over them hover putti holding a crown. On each side two Corinthian columns support a heavy classical cornice which scrapes against the ceiling. Between each pair of columns, there is a little seat with a strange canopy over it, made up of classical odds and ends. All this woodwork is not in its original position. John Evelyn, the 17th-century diarist, who saw it at Reigate in 1655, called it a Holbein fireplace and said that it had come from the house at Bletchingley, a few miles away, where Henry VIII had rusticated another of his wives, Anne of Cleves. That Holbein designed it now seems unlikely, and its original site is the subject of controversy;

25. Loseley House, Surrey. The whole composition is carved from a single block of clunch with remarkable technical skill. Heraldry, strapwork and classical features combine in a wild exuberance. It appears to be late Elizabethan, though Dr Pevsner wonders if this chimneypiece could have come, with other things in the house, from Henry VIII's Nonsuch Palace, and therefore be a very advanced design dating from about 1540. The iron work of the fire opening was made in the early 19th-century. The andirons are of Elizabethan design.

26. Longleat, Wiltshire. Surround and overmantel probably designed by Alain Maynard, *c.* 1575–80. Restrained in the chimneypiece part, but much more exuberant above, where the terms affectionately link arms and have bursting baskets of fruit on their heads. 19th-century grate and fender.

27. Burton Agnes Hall, Yorkshire, 1601–1610. An outstanding example of the grandest type of fireplace and overmantel of the Elizabethan period. Every type of architectural detail that can be thought of can be found in this chimneypiece which reaches the cornice of a hall, two storeys high. The top section from another house, Barmston. *c.* 1570.

what is beyond argument, however, is the fact that this example at Reigate is among the earliest of the great series of showpiece fireplaces which remained in fashion until the reign of James I.

Loseley House, also in Surrey, was built in 1561–69, and has in the drawing-room a huge chimneypiece and overmantel (Plate 25) carved out of one great block of clunch, a kind of chalk. (The house lies just below the chalk downs.) This unusual material, in the hands of a skilled craftsman, allows for beautifully crisp detail, which, in this particular example, the carver rendered in a total jumble of styles. There is a great deal of vermiculated rustication, that Renaissance ornament which looks as if toothpaste has been casually squeezed out and then petrified. There is neo-Anglo-Saxon interlacing, and also one or two little faces peeping out of the overmantel which look as if they had strayed from 18th-century Chinoiserie. Exuberant terms support the cornice at the top. Terms are half-figures which have tapering pedestals instead of legs and feet, and which are sometimes used to support cornices in classical and Renaissance architecture. Elizabethan designers were very fond of them, and treated them in any number of extravagant ways, either relying on their natural inventiveness, or making variations on the designs of a Netherlander, Vredeman de Vries.

A fireplace at Longleat (1567–75), possibly designed by a Frenchman, Alain Maynard (Plate 26), is more restrained than the Loseley one in its lower parts, but develops even more riotous terms at the top. The outer ones link arms; the centre one, by herself, ends in twisted tails, so that she looks like a skater frozen in a fast spin. Possibly the most engaging Elizabethan chimneypiece, certainly a good candidate for the most improper, architecturally, is the vast composition three tiers high, and spanning two storeys, at Burton Agnes Hall built between 1601 and 1610 (Plate 27). The Jacobean builder was responsible only for the fireplace surround and the central section, which has a bas-relief of the Wise and Foolish Virgins. The heraldic top section was removed from Barmston House (1570), and added, surprisingly, in

28. Hatfield House, Hertfordshire. Fireplace and overmantel designed as one composition in various coloured marbles by Maximilian Colt, 1608–12. The statue is of James I. The andirons, fireback, etc., although in Jacobean style, are Victorian replacements.

29. East Barsham Manor. Virtuoso brickwork chimneys of the Tudor period, *c.* 1520–30. It was usual to group them, with a standard shape but individual detail to each chimney. The chimneys taper sharply at the top, with only a small hole for the smoke.

1762. About this time, an 18th-century grate was added, but it has been removed since 1913.

After the beginning of James I's reign, taste in fireplaces became a little more restrained. They were still grandiose, but architectural motifs were used less wildly. A fine series can be seen at Hatfield (1607–11); here various coloured marbles were used together, and mosaic was even sent for from Venice. Many of these splendid fireplace compositions resemble the grandiloquent monuments which noblemen were erecting to themselves and their relations in churches and cathedrals. Maximilian Colt, who designed chimney-pieces at Hatfield, was a 'statuary' better known for his monuments than for his domestic designs; indeed his 'King James' fireplace at Hatfield (Plate 28), which has a portrait statue of the king standing above the mantel, would have done equally well for a monument to him, if a marble slab inscribed with a panegyric had replaced the fire opening.

It would be tedious to describe in detail more of these spectacular fireplaces, but they can be found and enjoyed in all parts of the country. Here is a short list. Prior to 1600 are Gilling Castle, Yorkshire, of about 1575; Canon Frome, late 16th-century; Montacute, Somerset, and Hardwick Hall, Derbyshire, of the 1590s. A large group, of stone, wood and plaster, belong to about 1600, among them Newburgh Priory, Yorkshire; Bradninch, Devon; Bisham Abbey, Berkshire; Cobham Hall, Kent; and, a particularly fine specimen, South Wraxall Manor, Wiltshire. Knole, Kent, of about 1605, Charlton House, also in Kent, of 1607, and New Place, Shedfield, Hampshire, of about 1623, carry the fashion through the reign of James I. East Quantoxhead, Somerset, was built late enough to have caryatids representing Red Indians (Pocahontas, the Red Indian princess who married an Englishman, was a well-known figure at the time) and, for variety, a bas-relief of the 'Entry into Jerusalem'. The last example, Lanhydrock, Cornwall, of the 1640s, takes us to within two years of the Civil War.

In the last chapter, we saw that round or octagonal chimneys were the usual shape of the medieval period. The development of brick-making led to the frequent use of brick for chimneys, and to some virtuoso brick-laying. The small, standard unit of the brick allowed the builder to satisfy his fancy with spiral-patterned chimneys, round, polygonal or square chimneys, chimneys with raised diaper patterns, and as many other types as he could invent. It seems to have been a point of honour that, if several chimneys were in a stack together, they should all be different. East Barsham Manor, a beautiful early Tudor house in Norfolk, has a splendid set of chimneys (Plate 29); its brickwork altogether is excellent. A pleasant hour can also be spent at Hampton Court studying the different designs of its chimneystacks; though almost all have been renewed, the replacements appear to be exact copies. An agreeable feature of Tudor and Elizabethan chimneys is that they usually finish at the top with a thickened frieze, or cap, which gives a good bold outline against the sky. A few inches below the cap there is often a projecting ring of brickwork, called the necking, and at the bottom of the chimney

30. Gainsborough Old Hall, Lincolnshire. Chimneystacks to 'lodgings' (suites of rooms) built by William Hickman. 1597–1600, in a wing added by him to the late 15th-century house. As well as the flues, the stacks contain cabinets and lavatories.

31. These chimneys at Wollaton Hall, Nottinghamshire, 1580–88, were designed by Robert Smythson to imitate – not very accurately – classical columns. The chimneypots are a later addition.

there is a solid base, sometimes stepped up in diminishing octagonal stages to the chimney shaft. All this makes the chimney into a fine, well-designed decorative feature of the house, as well as a practical necessity.

Not all chimneys were of this native design. Renaissance and Italian details can be found on the roof as well as downstairs in the hall or parlour. At Wollaton Hall, Nottinghamshire (1580–88), the chimneys designed by Robert Smythson are poor attempts at classical columns (Plate 31); and a further series of the same kind can be found at Burghley House, which is of about the same date. The architects, who had probably seen only illustrations of classical columns, detached from their proper background, may have been unaware that columns should be placed where they support, or seem to support an arch, entablature, or other architectural load.

3. The Caroline Period and the Later 17th Century

Robert Smythson's column chimneys could never have been designed by Inigo Jones. Inigo Jones had the advantage of several years' study in Italy, and was the first English architect who really understood Italian architecture. His buildings represent a complete break with the traditions which had developed in England from medieval times, and naturally his chimneypieces, like the rest of his architecture, are very different from what had gone before. It is a great pity that his houses have been so much altered that only at Wilton can we have any idea of what he thought appropriate in chimneypiece design. Even here the main work was carried out by John Webb, his pupil and relation by marriage, though the designs were made 'with the approbation' of the master, and no doubt under his influence. Inigo Jones's other domestic interiors either have no fireplaces at all, as in the case of the Banqueting House, Whitehall (which must have been intolerably cold even with braziers) or, like the Queen's House at Greenwich, have had them replaced. However, there is a splendid example in domestic style, in the Royal Pew, the Queen's Chapel, St James's Palace. An extant fireplace drawing by Jones is in the Wilton idiom.

Briefly, the main differences between the Elizabethan and Jacobean style of fireplace which we have recently considered, and that of Inigo Jones, is that the Elizabethan fireplace surround was made up of a number of architectural features stuck together, whereas the Inigo Jones chimneypiece, and its overmantel, were architectural features in themselves. Basically, the Inigo Jones fireplace is an interpretation of a Greek or Roman temple doorway. Columns stand on either side of the fire opening supporting an architrave, which forms the mantelshelf. Occasionally a pediment stands directly on the architrave but more usually a further pair of columns, or pilasters, architrave and pediment form an overmantel. The space between these upper columns could be used to hang a portrait, or later a mirror. The entire

32. Wilton House, Wiltshire. The Double Cube Room chimneypiece. Inigo Jones and John Webb at their most sumptuous. White marble chimneypiece, carved and gilded overmantel with inset painting; pendants of formalised flowers and fruit at the sides. Completed by 1652. The paintings by Van Dyck preceded the room by twenty years and the decoration was designed round them. Fireplace interior, grate and andirons Victorian.

33. Wilton House, Wiltshire. The Single Cube Room. One of a suite of rooms decorated in the Palladian style by the Webb-Jones partnership. The decorations were begun after 1647, and completed in the 1650s. Fireplace interior, grate and andirons Victorian.

ensemble was known in the 18th century as a 'continued chimneypiece', and Jones may also have used this description. Inigo Jones was singular in designing in this way in the first half of the 17th century (Lanhydrock was completed within seven or eight years of Wilton, and after the Queen's House) but this became the standard form for the fireplace in the 18th century, and we shall meet it, and its variations, again and again in the Palladian houses.

The six State rooms at Wilton, decorated by the Webb-Jones partnership, form one of the most splendid architectural suites in England. The chimneypieces are of white marble, and the overmantels white and gilt. Portraits are inset into the overmantels, and are flanked by swags and garlands, carved and gilded. The pediments are sometimes plain, but are often broken and scrolled. In the grandest room of all, the Double Cube Room, Van Dyck's portrait group of Charles's children is inset in

the overmantel, framed by gilded drapery and classical figures (Plate 32). In all this richness, however, the architectural elements still hold the compositions together. All the parts are in strict proportion, both to one another and to the carefully calculated measurements of the whole.

Two of these rooms show an interesting feature which will re-appear again and again. Until now, it was normal for the chimneypiece to be set flat on the wall. If the chimney could not be accommodated in the thickness of the wall, then it projected behind. Rufford Old Hall, which was built with a central hearth, but was given a wall fireplace sometime in the 16th century, shows this characteristic arrangement (Plate 9). In two of the rooms at Wilton, however, the Corner Room and the Colonnade Room, the chimneypieces, with their overmantels, are both set forward a foot or so from the wall. The cornice of the room breaks forward round the top of the overmantel, and so we have here what became a commonplace of later design, the chimney-breast projecting into the room. Not only was this more practical, since the chimney radiated its heat into the room, instead of wasting it on the air outside, but from the design point of view it also gave the designer certain advantages. He could regulate the proportions of his chimneybreast to complement, with a nice judgement, the proportions of his chimney-piece; and he also had a recessed space on each side which could be turned to good use. A shell-topped china cupboard could be inset, or a niche with a statue for the classically minded, or recessed bookcases for the studious.

The Civil War and the austerities which followed during the Commonwealth period did not encourage patrons to embark on elaborate building schemes, though John

34. Sydenham House, Devon. A design of 1656 added by Edward Wise to an already existing house. The low ceiling, combined with the old tradition of a composition stretching from floor to cornice, has resulted in odd proportions. Fireback and andirons probably contemporary.

Webb and Sir Roger Pratt carried on, so far as opportunity allowed, the Jones traditions. Building did not really begin again in earnest until the return of Charles II in 1660. By then, many people had changed to a new fuel for heating, and this greatly affected the design of fireplaces.

The earliest reference to a coal grate in the Oxford Dictionary is a quotation of 1605, 'A grate shall be layed wherein the coales of fire must lie'. Coal had been gradually coming into general use as a domestic fuel in Elizabethan times, though it had been known and used in some places for centuries. It was usually called 'sea-coal' both because useful quantities of it could be picked up on the north-east coast, washed in from the Durham and Northumberland seams below the sea, and also because Londoners, who made great use of it, got their coal by boat. As the forests, cut down for ship-building, houses, furniture and household equipment, as well as for fuel, rapidly dwindled away, coal provided a convenient alternative, particularly when Londoners, and people in other ports, could have it floated nearly to their doors. While country-dwellers went on using the traditional wood fire, with the logs propped up by andirons, lying on the 'down hearth' (that is, flat on the hearthstone), townspeople using coal had to adapt their fireplaces to a fuel which burned in a different way. Something was needed which would hold the coals together, and allow for some ventilation underneath. Hence the grate of our quotation. Its use in this context is new, but is merely an adaptation of a very old word 'grate' or 'grating', a criss-cross of iron bars used for windows, etc. For a coal fire, the grating was raised a little on short legs, provided with sides to prevent the coal falling out, and became a free-standing fire-basket. In fact it was a relation of the charcoal brazier which had long been known.

Considering that grates must have been in use from at least the beginning of the 17th century, it is extremely difficult to find early examples which can be dated accurately. Some fine examples which give a convincing effect, at Wilton and at Hatfield for instance, turn out on investigation to be Victorian. Grates were frequently changed in an effort to

35. Iron firepan overlaid with silver, with acanthus scrolls and the monogram of the Duke and Duchess of Lauderdale. Such firepans were used as charcoal-burners, though this one stands in a fireplace to which it obviously belongs, decorated with the same acanthus scrolls. Ham House, Surrey, *c.* 1675.

make the fire burn better, while the surrounding chimneypiece was left as it was. What seems to be a very early grate, though it may well have been used for logs as well as for coal, is at Haddon Hall in Derbyshire. It has a square firebasket with a pattern of alternating spearheads and fleur-de-lys on the front. The design is quite medieval in feeling, but is thought to date from the 16th century. The grate has only a front and sides, and needs to be pushed against a fireback, or the back wall of the fireplace. A free-standing oblong firebasket with horizontal bars on all four sides, and also believed to be of this period, is at Plas Mawr in Wales.

The first grate for which I have been able to

36. Bellows and hearth-brush with embossed silver decoration. Bought for Ham House, Surrey, by the Duke and Duchess of Lauderdale, *c.* 1675, and still in the house. The bellows, on which the Lauderdales' monogram can be seen, attracted Horace Walpole's attention when he visited Ham in the 18th century.

37. Iron shovels and tongs with applied silver ornament. Made for the Duke and Duchess of Lauderdale at Ham House, *c.* 1675, and still in the house.

38. Wrought iron andirons faced with cast and pierced brass ornament; the rosettes are formalised pots of tulips. Lyme Park, Cheshire, *c.* 1670.

39. Cast brass andiron with decoration in coloured enamels, and with the royal arms, *c.* 1670. Victoria and Albert Museum.

find a documented date is at Ham House, in Surrey. The house was altered in the 1670s and the large grate in the hall is mentioned in the inventory of 1679. As the fittings of the house have remained almost unaltered since and various fenders, bellows, andirons and other equipment can be identified from the inventory, it seems reasonable to suppose that this grate, too, is original. It is certainly a fairly primitive-looking piece, with heavy horizontal bars, and it is wedged into the fire opening with brick blocks, forming hobs, at the sides. Whether coal was burnt in it is not clear. Most of the other fireplaces have andirons and seem designed for burning wood, except those in two upstairs rooms, which have little silver-edged trays for burning charcoal (Plate 35). Wood was available from the estate, and coal may not have been considered an elegant

fuel. Certainly, if it had been the fashionable thing, the Lauderdales, who owned the house, would have equipped their fireplaces for burning it. They had everything of the latest model, so that Ham House gives us a perfect idea of a modish and expensive home of the time of Charles II (Plates 36, 37).

The fireplaces at Ham House, therefore, are well worth studying. They are much smaller than the other examples we have seen, probably to be in proportion to the small size of most of the rooms. Most of them are shallower from back to front than older examples, and the hearth inside the fire opening, instead of being oblong in plan, is D-shaped. To left and right, inside, there is a curved wall covered with white glazed tiles which are thought to be original (Plate 40). The tiles do not go all the way round the interior of the fireplace;

41

40. Ham House, Surrey. The chimneypiece design can probably be attributed to Francis Cleyn. The room was decorated in 1637. The white tiles inside the fireplace opening are also thought to be 17th-century, but a little later, the later 1670s when the Lauderdales redecorated the house. The andirons are also of this period.

41. Ham House, Surrey. Fireplace with marble bolection moulding, wood surround, and carved overmantel decoration. The painting is inset in an elaborately carved frame flanked by drops of fruit and leaves in distant imitation of Grinling Gibbons. The tiles and hearth are believed to be original; late 1670s. Grate later.

at the centre stands an iron fireback, attractively embossed with an heraldic or classical design, and above this there is a vertical black strip of either metal or well-sooted plaster. The fashion for such tiles may have originated in Holland, where tin-glazed tiles, ornamented with blue pseudo-oriental patterns, were used for kitchens, skirtings and all sorts of domestic purposes. The Ham House tiles appear to be tin-glazed and could perhaps have been products of the Lambeth factory, established in the 1660s; water transport up the Thames would have been easy.

Another interesting feature of the Ham

House fireplaces is the arrangement of the hearths. As the fire was made directly on the hearth inside the fire opening, this inner area had of course to be a working surface of stone. This working surface, however, does not extend into the room as a modern hearth does. It stops at the fire opening, in line with the wall. Beyond this line, in the room itself, there is another, decorative, hearth made of a material to match or harmonise with the chimneypiece surround. A dark red marble surround, for instance, has a 'show' hearth of the same marble. A black marble surround has a 'show' hearth in diamonds of black and white marble. Where a fender has survived, as it has in the Miniature Room on the first floor, it is set along the join between the working and the 'show' hearths. As it was propped up at each end by the jambs of the fireplace, it is quite straight. It was only later, when it was put round the hearth inside the room, that the fender needed to be self-supporting, and took on its familiar shape, with returns at the sides.

A number of the Ham House fireplaces have surrounds of bolection moulding (Plate 41), a neat and modest way of decorating the fire opening which was fashionable in the later 17th and early 18th centuries. This style has no architectural pretensions, no columns and no architrave. It simply treats the fire opening as if it were a picture, and frames it with a

42. Thorney Abbey, Cambridgeshire. Bolection-moulded design of 1660, set in a woodwork surround which covers the whole of the chimneybreast, and repeats scrolls and mouldings which occur elsewhere in the panelling of the room. Early 20th-century grate.

43. Chatsworth, Derbyshire. The State Dining-room. This part of the house was designed by William Talman, 1687–96. The plain bolection moulding surrounding the fire opening is surmounted by a wreath of virtuoso woodcarving in the Grinling Gibbons manner, but carried out by the local craftsman, Samuel Watson. Inside the wreath there is a panel of parquetry, with a small portrait inset. Variations of this unusual combination of carving, parquetry and portrait appear in the other State rooms.

wide, fat moulding, identical at the top and sides (Plate 42). A broad moulding of this kind, made of marble (as at Ham House, Groombridge Place, Belton House, or many other late 17th-century mansions) looks very handsome indeed. It had, however, one dis-

advantage. Bolection moulding is thick at its inner edge, but dwindles to an inch or so at the outer edge. Nothing could be balanced on this narrow ledge; but the vogue, again coming from Holland, was to have blue and white oriental porcelain pots (or Delft or Lambeth imitations) ranged in rows wherever possible—on the cornices of cupboards, on ledges or on mantelshelves. A separate shelf therefore was often fixed a few inches above the fireplace to accommodate this essential *garniture de cheminée*. Several can be seen at Ham House.

One type of chimneypiece, popular in the late 17th century, which had plenty of display space, was set across the corner of a room. In the next room, the fireplace was put across the adjacent corner. Instead of going straight up, the flues were often sloped, leaving a receding surface above the fireplace which could be fitted with shelves or brackets. Ham House and Hampton Court Palace have examples of this kind, and there is a very late one (of the 18th century) at Mereworth Castle (Plate 65). Such overmantels were ideal for displaying the oriental china which fashionable ladies were beginning to collect.

Inigo Jones inset paintings in the overmantels of his fireplaces, and this continued to be a popular way of showing off paintings, especially family portraits. At Chatsworth, rather small portraits are set in octagonal surrounds of veneer, edged with extremely skilfully carved garlands of flowers and fruit (Plate 43). These were long thought to have been carved by Grinling Gibbons, until evidence came to light that they had been carved on the estate. Grinling Gibbons's virtuoso skill, which could shape limewood into flowers and leaves as delicate as if they had been made of feathers, set a standard which many craftsmen strove to attain. Genuine Gibbons carving decorates a number of chimneypieces, notably at Petworth, where portraits are linked together in pairs by airy trails of birds and plants. It is interesting to compare the Gibbons style of chimneypiece which has fragile, naturalistic flowers dropping on each side of a portrait (Plate 44), with the garlands falling on each side of the portrait in Inigo Jones's Double Cube Room at Wilton. Here the robust, architectural flowers do not pretend to be anything else but wood.

A further piece of overmantel decoration which is still with us today came into use in the late 17th century. John Evelyn first saw looking-glasses being made at Vauxhall in 1676, and overmantel looking-glasses are thought to date from the 1680s and 1690s. Only small pieces of mirror glass could then be made, and the width of the fireplace had to be spanned by three or more pieces of glass. No serious attempt seems to have been made in these early days to cover the joins with moulding, or to make them into a decorative feature, and they were not considered in any way a disfigurement. Most of these early mirrors were a horizontal oblong, but by the beginning of the 18th century, the fashionable shape had become a vertical oblong, still formed of two or more pieces. The price of large pieces of mirror glass remained very high until well on in the 18th century; a mirror could cost £50, while a 'fine

44. Belton House, Lincolnshire. Corner chimneypiece with marble fireplace, and pendants of fruit and flowers naturalistically carved in the Grinling Gibbons style by Edward Carpenter, flanking an inset portrait. 1685–90.

wallnut tree table' in the same bill cost £4 10s.

By the mid-17th century, the exuberance of the early brickwork chimneys was considerably moderated. Chimneys would be grouped in sets, all matching, and with the square shafts set diamondwise. Later, the design was simplified still more, and the flues, six or more, would be fused together into one large solid rectangular stack. In a small house, one of these stacks might form the centrepiece of the weighty hipped roof. In larger houses the stacks were set symmetrically wherever possible, and often at either end of the house. The faces of these stacks were often decorated with recessed panels, with a stone coping round the top. At Winslow Hall (1700), the only house, I believe, which can confidently be associated with Sir Christopher Wren, four great chimneystacks stand in line along the flat centre of the hipped roof, crowning the house in a dignified manner (Plate 46).

With coal fires, getting rid of the smoke became a problem, and this may well have been the reason why people kept to wood fires while they could. Fireplaces became

46. A stately row of chimneystacks, of red brick with stone caps, on the roof of Winslow Hall, Buckinghamshire, 1700.

45. The Queen's House, Greenwich. Chimney in Palladian style designed by Inigo Jones, 1616–35.

smaller, and flues narrower, to deal with the hotter fire of the new fuel, but combustion was poor. As early as 1661, Evelyn wrote a paper called *Fumifugium*, in which he investigated means of restricting 'this horrid smoake' hanging over London from the coal fires, a problem which proved insoluble until the mid-20th century. Prince Rupert, who was an extremely versatile inventor, to whom we owe a metal alloy (prince's metal), the process of mezzo-tinting, and possibly 'Prince Rupert's drops', those strange glass tadpoles which embody the principle now used in making toughened glass, turned his mind also to the problem of smoky fireplaces. He invented a system by which the smoke was first directed backwards and then down behind the fireback, before being allowed to go up the chimney. The metal baffle, round which the smoke was meant to take its hairpin bend, had to be removable, so that the chimney could be swept. Prince Rupert does not seem to have taken sufficiently into account the fact that hot air rises. Much of the smoke, instead of threading its way round the various obstacles, must have gone straight out into the room, and I do not think it likely that the baffles, once removed, would often have been put back again.

4. The Queen Anne and Earlier Georgian Period

47. Castle Howard, Yorkshire. In this chimney-piece in the hall, Sir John Vanbrugh reached the limits of English domestic Baroque. It was designed by 1700, but not completed until 1712. Fireplace interior altered later.

The English never took to the Baroque with any great enthusiasm. They were happy to be remembered, after death, by great grandiloquent memorials ('Man is a noble animal, splendid in ashes and pompous in the grave'), and we should be the poorer without the theatrical baroque inventions of Scheemakers or Roubiliac. But the home was quite another thing; it had to be lived in, and most patrons continued to prefer the comfort of the style evolved in the late 17th century, rather than the draughty splendours of a baroque mansion.

Truly baroque chimneypieces are therefore as rare as the rooms appropriate to them, but fortunately a few adventurous patrons employed Sir John Vanbrugh, the architect who carried English Baroque to its farthest limits. In the hall at Castle Howard, there is perhaps the most successful baroque chimneypiece in Britain (Plate 47). The room spans two storeys; a passage threads its way round at first-floor level and opens out into a kind of tribune or open gallery above the chimneypiece. The overmantel therefore rises up into space, and the statues on the top stand out against a shadowy background. Vanbrugh's ingenuity has got rid of the flue, which would normally rise up behind the overmantel; presumably it has been sharply angled to left or right, and into the wall at one side, in a way fairly common in France, but extremely rare in England.

Vanbrugh's dramatic imagination can be seen too, at the opposite end of the fireplace complex. By the end of the 17th century, as we have seen, chimneystacks had tidied themselves into solid, symmetrical blocks of masonry or brick, to be set at the ends of the house, or ranged in a solemn row along the roof. But it needed Vanbrugh to think of crowning King's Weston House, near Bristol, with chimneystacks connected by arcades (Plate 48). The conception is no doubt just as odd as Smythson's column chimneystacks, but there is no denying the dignity of the effect. Before chimneypots were allowed to

48. King's Weston, Somerset. Chimneys arranged in a dignified arcade by Sir John Vanbrugh, 1713–1725. The chimneypots are later.

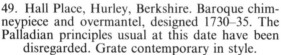

49. Hall Place, Hurley, Berkshire. Baroque chimneypiece and overmantel, designed 1730–35. The Palladian principles usual at this date have been disregarded. Grate contemporary in style.

50. Palladian chimneypiece design. Plate 13 of *Some Designs of Mr. Inigo Jones and Mr. William Kent* (1744), by John Vardy.

spike the skyline, it must have appeared as if a section of a Roman aqueduct had alighted on the roof.

If customers were resistent to the Baroque, it was possible, by the beginning of the Georgian period, to sell them an equally inconvenient style, the Palladian. The Inigo Jones style of the first half of the 17th century was based on that of Palladio, who lived in northern Italy in the 16th century. Both Inigo Jones and Palladio, however, had to wait until the 1720s to be fully appreciated in England. They then became twin architectural gods. Though Colen Campbell built the first Palladian buildings, the chief populariser of the style was Lord Burlington, who gathered round himself a group of architects and designers of whom William Kent probably is the best known (Plate 50). Between them they set out to reform the old-fashioned taste of their contemporaries, re-working themes from Palladio and Jones. At Boynton Hall, Yorkshire, for instance, there is a chimneypiece of about 1730 (probably by William Kent) which is based on one of Inigo Jones's designs for Somerset House (Plate 51). Lord Burlington's chimneypieces at Chiswick House are similar.

Preferably, the true Palladian chimneypiece

51. Boynton Hall, Yorkshire. Chimneypiece with details taken from Inigo Jones's designs for Somerset House. Stone. Probably by William Kent, *c.* 1730. A 'Chimney Piece at Sir William Stricklands,' by Kent appeared in Isaac Ware's *Designs of Inigo Jones and others* (1743). Sir William consulted Lord Burlington in altering his house, Boynton Hall.

was made of white marble, an expensive material imported also for memorial sculptures, and often carved by the same 'statuaries' and masons. Sometimes the well-to-do patron, requiring an impressive display for his most splendid room, would commission an overmantel as well as a chimneypiece of marble, and would go to the expense of employing such a sculptor as Rysbrack to carve it for him. Rysbrack's magnificent reliefs of Roman subjects (a compliment to the classical education of his patrons) can be seen at Houghton (Plate 52), Woburn Abbey (Plate 53), and Clandon Park. Such panels as these could be set in architectural surrounds carved by less gifted craftsmen. But where figures as well as architectural motifs were required, as in the splendidly pompous chimneypieces with classical caryatids or terms at each side, an artist of Rysbrack's stature, or one of his

slightly less distinguished colleagues, Van Nost (Plate 54), Cheere or Scheemakers, would be called in to carve the whole composition.

These caryatid figures, according to Isaac Ware in *The Complete Body of Architecture* (1756), had to be managed judiciously. The Persian [male] figure should 'have a look of indignation or contempt, and the Caryatick, or woman, of dejection without pain. Let the Persian seem to say that he does not feel the load but the indignity; and the Caryatick that she understands her position with humility'. The architect should be careful to use only male figures for 'continued chimneypieces'. 'The female figures . . . are to stand at seeming ease, and it would be monstrous to load them with ornament up to the ceiling'. Care had also to be taken to see that the hands and feet of the figures were so placed that delicate fingers and toes could not be damaged by 'servants managing the fewel'. Finally, there was the problem of draping the caryatids, since 'we banish anatomy from the parlour of the polite gentleman'. It is a pity we have no record of the gentleman's reaction to the contemptuous stare of his well-dressed caryatids.

The chimneypiece settled down into a standard form, based on the principles brought here by Inigo Jones. As we have seen, the sides of the chimneypiece represented classical columns, the lintel represented their entablature. To break up the long line of this entablature, an oblong plaque, known in the 18th century as a 'tablet', was frequently set in the middle (Plate 55). This offered room for the portrayal of a small classical scene. If there was an overmantel, it repeated the same units over again though without columns, which would be 'too massy and uncouth'. Sometimes a pediment crowned the whole structure. The elegant relation of the two parts to each other distinguished the talented from the mediocre designer. 'Many', said Ware in scorn, 'think that a continued chimneypiece is a simple one with something on top of it. Some flutter of ornament and some shape of a frame, they suppose are needful on this occasion, but further they seem not to have carried their researches'.

49

52. Chimneypiece and overmantel in the Marble Parlour at Houghton Hall, Norfolk. Both the relief of a sacrifice scene and the architectural surround were carved by the sculptor Michael Rysbrack, who was working on it in 1732. The original cartoon (unique in being the only full-scale drawing of a relief of this period) was at Houghton until 1851, and is now in the British Museum. William Kent designed the interior decoration of this house in the grandest Palladian style. Grate contemporary in style.

53. Woburn Abbey, Bedfordshire. Relief panel carved by Michael Rysbrack in 1755, and inset in a chimneypiece and overmantel surround carved by John Deval. The Duke of Bedford provided his own stone for the bas-relief, and paid Rysbrack 100 guineas for it. Deval supplied Tottenhoe and Portland stone for his part of the design, and was paid £94. The relief is identical in design to that supplied by Rysbrack (in marble) for the overmantel in the Stone Hall at Houghton Hall, *c.* 1730. Grate early 19th-century.

54. Hampton Court Palace. The Queen's Gallery. Bolection-moulded chimneypiece, with overmantel carved by John van Nost (or Ost) in 1700, for which he was paid £30. The influence of Grinling Gibbons can be seen in the carving of the flower garlands and the doves. The fireback, embossed with the royal arms, is probably contemporary with the chimneypiece.

55. Biggin Hall, Northamptonshire. Late 18th-century chimneypiece carved in marble, with darker marble used in the frieze. An almost exact copy of the central tablet can be found in a chimneypiece at Everingham Park, Yorkshire.

56. Much Hadham Hall, Hertfordshire. A simple but pleasant chimneypiece with a slightly projecting chimneybreast. The present painting is smaller than the original. The house was built in 1735, possibly by John James. The andirons are of an earlier type.

Even when there were no actual columns or pilasters, their ghostly presence was felt in the proportions of the details, so that there were sections corresponding to the base, the shaft and the capital.

In the hands of the Palladian school, therefore, the design of the chimneypiece was serious and architectural. Even when quite simple, as in the example shown from Much Hadham Hall (Plate 56), it could have great dignity; the more elaborate designs often reach real grandeur. Nothing, however, could make it either intimate or light-hearted. The Palladian architect needed room to manoeuvre, and there was no means by which he could shrink his designs down to a scale appropriate for a small house. The designs, too, were suitable for rooms for formal occasions, not for casual everyday life (Plate 57). Ware makes it clear that a 'continued chimneypiece' could only be used where there are other sculptured details in the room, and where the walls are panelled or plastered. For a papered or silk-hung room they were out of the question, for 'what could be so mean as the thought of framing a piece of hanging?' The principles of Palladianism were hardly questioned for most of the 18th century, but increasingly, as time went on, the householder

57. Mawley Hall, Shropshire. Designed *c.* 1730, probably by Francis Smith of Warwick. Instead of an overmantel with architectural motifs there is a superb trophy of arms and Roman armour. The frieze of the chimneypiece is ornamented with astronomical instruments, intertwined with flowers.

58. Gateley Hall, Norfolk. Rococo plasterwork overmantel, *c*. 1750, with a rustic scene surrounded by scrolls and flowers.

kept his true Palladianism for the outside of his house, and experimented with something less solemn inside.

The Chimneypiece Maker's Daily Assistant, a design manual published in 1766 and including the work of a number of designers, shows standard Palladian designs, but also all sorts of more lively informal schemes. In France, a new style – Rococo – had appeared, and by the middle of the century this fresh approach towards interior decoration had become more and more fashionable and a welcome change from strict Palladianism. Rococo is essentially a light lacy style, evading strict symmetry wherever possible and making great use of such motifs as delicate flowers and fluttering ribbons. Such decoration could be carved in wood or moulded in plaster (Plate 58) by the skilled *stuccadores* who came from Italy to find a living in this country. A good example of this style is at Combe, in Devonshire. The chimneypiece is of about 1760 and is based on a Chippendale

design (Plate 59). Serpentine lines are used wherever possible. Hogarth was reflecting the popular taste when he referred to the serpentine, or ogee, as 'the line of beauty'. Foliage, flowers and a bird's nest are carved in pinewood under the mantelshelf. The overmantel mirror is oval, and is surrounded by a froth of delicate decoration, from which coil scroll candle brackets. By this time the fire opening was usually outlined by slips of marble, whatever the material used for the actual chimneypiece. Here the marble slips also follow the serpentine line. The whole ensemble is as far as it can be from the formality of the standard Palladian chimneypiece. Not all designers went so far; some designed serious Palladian

59. Combe, Devon. Carved pine rococo chimneypiece and overmantel incorporating a mirror. The marble inner slip follows the curved line of the lintel. Candle brackets curve out from the woodwork. The design includes a bird's nest, Chinese ho-ho birds, and a little mouse looking at itself in the glass. There may originally have been a freestanding rococo cast iron grate. *c*. 1760.

60. Farnborough Hall, Warwickshire. A Palladian composition with rococo detailing. A painting by Pannini of the Campidoglio in Rome is framed in the overmantel. Other paintings by Pannini are framed in more exuberant rococo plasterwork round the room. *c*. 1750. Early 19th-century grate and fender.

chimneypieces, and then relaxed into rococo frolics for the overmantels (Plate 60).

Even the most enthusiastic classicists relaxed their principles from time to time. After a long period of total denigration, medieval architecture was beginning to be noticed and even occasionally appreciated once more. The word Gothic, which originally had meant simply 'barbarian', was beginning to acquire overtones of romance. It was usually at this time spelt 'Gothick' and I shall spell it in this way when referring to 18th century sham medievalism, to distinguish this from the much more accurate reconstructions of the Gothic style belonging to the 19th century and, of course, from genuine medieval Gothic.

Even such a devoted Palladian as William Kent occasionally deviated into Gothick, and Horace Walpole made himself the champion of a style characterised by enthusiasm for, rather than knowledge of, the medieval past. By the middle of the 18th century, a small but steady trickle of Gothick designs had begun to flow from the pens of architects (Plate 61). An interesting example, whose early date is known as it is in a tower erected in 1746 to commemorate Culloden, has a handsome standard 18th-century chimneypiece. Above it, however, there rests an ogee-topped overmantel, intended to suggest the 14th century, which culminates in three pinnacles. Walpole's own house, Strawberry Hill, intended as a model for Gothick students, just as Lord Burlington's Chiswick House had been

61. Gothick chimneypiece designs from *The Universal System of Household Furniture* (1762) by Ince and Mayhew. Note the firedogs instead of a grate, to give a more medieval effect.

62. Arbury Hall, Warwickshire. Sir Roger New-digate's Gothick. He used a Westminster Abbey tomb for a model, that of Aymer de Valence (1324). An 18th-century grate decorated with the medieval motifs. No model existed for a medieval fender, and the one here is of normal late 18th-century style. Designed in 1762 by Henry Keene. Late 18th-century pole firescreens at each side.

intended as a model for Palladian students thirty years earlier, contains some interesting chimneypieces, the designs based on tombs and sedilia which had appealed to Walpole in his cathedral walks. Perhaps the most elaborate of all the Gothick chimneypieces can be found in the house of Sir Roger Newdigate, an admirer of classical antiquity who came home from the Grand Tour laden with copies of Roman sculptures, but who nevertheless gothicised Arbury Hall from top to bottom. One fireplace is based on the tomb of Aymer

de Valence in Westminster Abbey (Plate 62).

Another style which provided a relief from Palladianism was Chinoiserie—as inaccurate as Gothick, yet with something of the same fragile charm. Chinese porcelain had been imported for a century or so, and we have seen how it became a necessary part of mantel-shelf decoration in the time of Charles II and William and Mary. Chinese wallpaper was also imported, and lacquer chests from China and Japan. Decorators were therefore familiar with a repertoire of motifs—mandarins, gnarled trees, peachblossom, fretwork fences—and used them to decorate furniture and other household requirements. Customers with Chinese wallpaper demanded chinoiserie fire-places to match (Plate 63); and, since no models existed, the designers invented their own, of a kind of rococo scattered with details intended to strike a Chinese note. Faces with slit eyes and drooping moustaches, pagodas and long-necked creatures known as ho-ho birds appear wherever possible, mixed up with genuine Chinese ware, since almost every design of this type included little scroll brackets on which the collector could place his own porcelain bowls, vases and mandarin figures. At Claydon House, Buckinghamshire, there is a complete Chinese room, specially for taking tea in, with a pavilion, overdoors full of Chinese faces, and nonsensical fire-places (Plate 64). Nobody took any of this seriously. A writer in *The World* (1753) remarked that 'not one in a thousand of all the stiles, gates, rails, pales, temples, chimney-pieces, etc., etc., etc., which are called Chinese has the least resemblance to anything that China ever saw; nor would an English church be a less uncommon sight to a travelling mandarin than an English pagoda'.

The dedicated Palladian came up against difficulties when designing chimneys. Palladio had designed his houses for summer use in the Veneto, where heating was unnecessary, so that few real Palladian models existed. The cognoscenti might be, as Pope said,

'Proud to take cold at a Venetian door,
Conscious they act the true, Palladian part,
And though they starve, [freeze] they starve
by rules of Art'

but they could not freeze all the time. As we

63. Chinoiserie chimneypiece from *The Universal System of Household Furniture* (1762) by Ince and Mayhew. Alternative details are shown. The grate is also in Chinese style.

64. Claydon House, Buckinghamshire. Chinoiserie fireplace in the Chinese Room. The superb rococo carving in this and other rooms in the house was executed by Luke Lightfoot, between 1757 and 1769. Dr Lindsay Boynton (*Furniture History*, Vol. II, 1966) has found evidence that the specious rogue Lightfoot obtained over £30,000 from Earl Verney for decorations valued at about £7,000.

65. Mereworth Castle, Kent. Designed by Colen Campbell, 1722–25. An elaborately carved and gilded chimneypiece in the dining-room. Here, as in the other rooms at the angles of this house, the chimneypiece had to be in the inner corner, nearest to the dome, so that the flues could curve up the dome and eject the smoke through the cupola on top. Late 18th-century grate.

have seen, Jones, and the 18th-century Palladians after him, evolved an acceptable design for the chimneypiece and overmantel, following classical principles. This looked well inside, and did not affect the design of the exterior. Chimneys were another matter. On occasion, heroic measures were taken. At Chiswick, the chimneys are disguised as the obelisks Palladio occasionally used to emphasise the corners of his buildings. At Mereworth Castle (Plate 65), the flues curve up the dome, and let the smoke out from the little cupola on the top. Where the chimney-stacks could not be disposed of, they were made as unobtrusive as possible. The Palladian roof was as flat as could be managed (following the Italian model), and was frequently further hidden behind a balustrade or cornice, so that the chimneys, which were

as short as possible, did not show much. In town terrace houses, which were being built at this time in their hundreds, stacks were frequently contrived in the party walls between the houses. From a distance, they provided a rhythmical vertical motif, which marked the division between one house and the next. The stack, which now had the flues arranged one behind the other, was deep from back to front and rather flat. It was beginning to look untidy, as the chimneypots, which were originally a draught device fitted into the top of the flue inside the stack, now appeared on top of it, in all their variety of shape, dictated by the theories, fancy or desperation of the householder. Robert Clavering in his *Essay on Chimneys* (1779) illustrates a variety of chimneypots. One looks like an animal with its mouth open.

5. The Later Georgian Period

The excavations at Herculaneum, a city buried in 79 AD after an eruption of Vesuvius, provided new ideas on classical interior decoration. Here was a style, indubitably Roman, which did not take its classicism too seriously. Adaptations of it seemed much more appropriate to Palladian interiors than the rococo designs, or the Chinese and Gothic schemes that had recently been popular. It was more suitable than even the heavy Palladian style itself, based as it was on those large-scale architectural elements belonging to the exteriors of classical buildings which had been robust enough to survive the weathering of fifteen centuries. Robert Adam, who returned to England from Italy in 1758, was the first to popularise the new style, and soon all branches of interior decoration felt what Sir John Soane called 'the electric power of this revolution in art'. For the standard Palladian motifs, Adam substituted what he called 'a beautiful variety of light mouldings, gracefully formed, delicately enriched, and arranged with propriety and skill'.

One of the features of Adam's work was a type of ornamental decoration which was derived from Roman originals. He called this 'grotesque', and explained why: 'By grotesque is meant that beautiful light style used by the Romans in the ornament of their palaces, baths and villas . . . The Italians give to ruins dug up and cleared the name of "grotto" . . . hence the modern word "grotesque".' Characteristic of his decorative work are the spidery, low-relief trails and scrolls, which he called 'the flowing *rainceau*', and the oval or round medallions with bas-reliefs of classical figures.

A further step away from the severe classical style was the introduction of colour into chimneypiece designs. There had, of course, previously been designs in marble of two or more colours; examples can be found dating from the reign of Elizabeth, and they even occur in the work of architects of the Palladian School. Again Adam was inspired by Roman originals, for he much admired the decorative schemes consisting of a variety of pale colours relieved with white ornament. This offended the purists, like Sir William Chambers, who thought that only white marble was suitable. Adam himself was prepared to use unrelieved white marble at times, when he was working on a grand scale, as in the Great Hall at Kedleston Hall, but for smaller and more intimate rooms preferred polychrome decoration.

Many of these polychrome chimneypieces were executed in a medium, more delicate and flexible than marble, called scagliola. Scagliola is a composite substance made up of powdered lime, gypsum and marble dust, held together with an adhesive, which when hard can be polished to give a remarkable and hard-wearing imitation of marble. As its name shows, it is an Italian invention, and Italian craftsmen, skilled for centuries in mosaic work, were remarkably adept in its use. The earliest scagliola work in this country is probably the chimneypiece surround, with its matching hearth, at Ham House; it seems likely that this was imported from Italy, though it was designed specially and incorporates the Lauderdales' monogram. After this, I believe that scagliola was rarely used until Adam brought back from Italy a craftsman called Bartoli, who was a virtuoso performer in this medium. For Adam, he made a number of chimneypieces of marble inset with coloured decorations in scagliola. In 1773, for instance, he carried out Adam's design for a chimneypiece at 20 St James's Square, London (where it still remains) ornamented with lions' heads and ivy trails in natural colours. Trails or *rainceaux* or classical scenes of goddesses and nymphs in appropriate colour schemes constitute the usual ornamentation of a chimneypiece by Bartoli, and the Adam drawings at the Soane Museum, London, indicate that such designs were frequently supplied. Further examples of this kind of fireplace can be seen at Syon House and Osterley Park, both in Middlesex, and at Home House, Portman Square (Plates 66, 67).

It is customary to call chimneypieces of this

66. Chimneypiece in the Etruscan style by Robert Adam for Home House, 20 Portman Square, London. Drawing dated 1775 in the Soane Museum, London.

67. Chimneypiece in Home House, 20 Portman Square. Apart from the fact that the medallions at the corners are circles in squares, instead of plain squares, the design repeats exactly the drawing shown in Plate 66 by Robert Adam. The chimneypiece is executed in scagliola work on marble, probably by Bartoli. The grate appears to be a copy of a characteristic design of the Adam period; the fender is also of Adam style. Curved fenders were called 'compassed'.

polychrome type 'Bossi work', since an Italian called Bossi made a number of such chimneypieces in Dublin in the 1780s and 1790s. However, if somebody's name must be attached to the style, I think it should be that of Bartoli since he was working in this medium, under Adam, at least a decade earlier.

Experiments were also carried out in painting on marble, and Angelica Kauffmann, an early Royal Academician often employed by Adam, tried her hand at painting a marble chimneypiece at Bradwell Lodge, Essex. It appears to have been done in oils. Another experiment was carried out by the potter Josiah Wedgwood, who, from the 1770s, was able to supply tablets (the central oblong plaques) and blocks (the medallions for the outer corners) in his basalt (black) and jasper (blue and white or green and white) stoneware which could be inset in wood or marble chimneypieces. Many have survived until today. By 1786 he was able to build up the whole front of a chimneypiece out of jasper plaques, held in a marble framework (Plate 68). At least seven of these were made of which six can be traced.

The Adam style of ornament, with low relief trails, and oval or round medallions, could of course be carved in wood, but a satisfactory and less expensive substitute could be contrived by using ready-made moulded detail. The most usual medium was plaster, which Adam himself often used, diverting one of his brilliant plasterers, such as Joseph Rose, from work on walls or ceilings to the decoration of chimneypieces. Plasterwork, which was fragile, needed a specialist to do it, and for people who could not get the services of one, other media were available.

Matthew Boulton, who was, among many other things, a highly skilled die-stamper, made a certain number of decorative details for walls, doors and chimneypieces in moulded pewter. The pewter, of course, was not meant to show, but was painted to blend in with the background. The Victoria and Albert Museum has a wood chimneypiece of this kind, unpainted, so that the pewter decoration can be seen; it dates from about the 1770s. Wedgwood, a friend of Boulton, remarked that Boulton and his partner Fothergill were

68. Marble chimneypiece inset with Wedgwood plaques in blue and white jasper ware. The designs for the central plaque and the Medusa heads were by John Flaxman, c. 1786. Originally at Longton Hall, Staffordshire, now at the Lady Lever Art Gallery, Cheshire.

making such decorations die-stamped in tin. Wedgwood was an able chemist, and it seems unlikely that he would have mistaken pewter for tin; however, I believe that no tin specimens have come to light so far. They would only be visible, of course, when the wall, chimneypiece, or other decorated item was completely stripped of paint; otherwise they would be indistinguishable from wood or plaster.

Another medium for making decorative details was invented by Mrs Eleanor Coade. In her factory near the site of Waterloo Station, London, Mrs Coade made an imitation stone which has never been satisfactorily copied, though its composition is known. It was a ceramic body, and probably the temperature and firing time were critical and have not yet been re-discovered. The result was a material which looked like stone, but unlike most natural stones, was impervious to the chemicals in the atmosphere. Many decorative features, such as capitals and figures intended to ornament the exterior of a building, as well as funerary monuments and fountains, were designed by the best contemporary sculptors and made in her factory. She also made – and this is what concerns us here – a most elaborate and varied series of decorative

ornaments and motifs, which could be bought separately and assembled by the craftsman in any way he pleased. Trails of husks for instance, essential details of the Adam style, could be bought ready-made, or assembled, husk by husk, for a few pence a dozen. Medallions and *paterae* (rosette-shaped ornaments) used at the time in vast quantities, cost a shilling or so. A more elaborate detail, a plaque for instance, might be several shillings. She even sold terms four feet high for the sides of chimneypieces, at two guineas. For those who did not want the trouble of working out their own designs, she sold chimneypieces ready-made. Some were entirely of Coade stone, including an impressive one with an anchor, cables and seaweed, and Ionic capitals composed of dolphins, which must have been designed with an admiral in mind – Howe, Hood or Rodney perhaps. Others were of wood with Coade stone ornaments. The grandest could cost up to £40, and were no cheaper than marble, but tiny ones, for a dressing-room or a garret, could be had for as little as 25s.

Other competitors were also in the field. Messrs Ewines and Rostell of Birmingham, who had what must have been, in view of 18th-century mortality rates, a good steady trade in coffin ornaments, also made metal decorative details from which almost any design could be made up, and which they advertised as being the cheapest available. It has not so far been possible to investigate whether this claim is likely to have been true.

Design books abounded, so that the village carpenter could turn out a chimneypiece, with the help of these ready-made details, as fashionably as the London man. Such a writer as James Pain, for instance, wrote *The Builder's Golden Rule, The Practical House Carpenter,* and *The British Palladio.* That this last book was not published until 1797 shows how long Palladianism was a living force. Pain was particularly helpful on chimneypieces in *The Carpenter's and Joiner's Repository,* where he gave a table showing how the chimneypiece could be proportioned to the room, giving specimen sizes for rooms from 12 to 36 feet square. (For oblong rooms, you added the length of a long and a short

69. Illustration from *The Chimneypiece Maker's Daily Assistant* (1766). The bust of Inigo Jones watches the proceedings.

side together and halved the result.) He explained 'for every six Inches in the Bigness of the Room, add one Inch to the Width of the Chimney and one quarter Inch to the Height'. This rule, which he failed to keep with any accuracy in the specimens given, produces some rather odd proportions in the smaller sizes, but it is interesting that they should be supplied at all in a work designed for the simple carpenter. The local craftsman was also instructed carefully that the architrave was to be one-seventh part or one-eighth part of the opening, and the cornice two-thirds or three-quarters of the architrave; he was expected to have thoroughly digested these classical terms.

In another book, *The Builder's Golden Rule* (1782), Pain gave equally careful instructions for costing marble chimneypieces, and this is an indication that they would have been required for the good middle class house as well as for the luxurious mansion. Statuary marble cost 30s. per cubic foot. Labour, in relation to the cost of the materials, was cheap enough: 7s. per foot super (measurement by length) for moulded work. For less affluent customers, he quoted 'New bastard statuary marble' at 6s. per foot, which may perhaps, at this cheap price, have been some form of scagliola.

Pain gave complete details of a house costing £1,534 0s. 1d., which included a dining-room chimneypiece for the striking figure of £45. As money in the late 18th century was worth approximately twelve times what it is today, this fine decorative feature cost the equivalent of well over £500. By comparison, the 'best parlour' chimneypiece, at £36, was more reasonable. This may not have been because the room was less splendid, but because large-scale designs, cutting into more marble, were thought more suitable for dining-rooms than the more delicate, flatter relief appropriate to sitting-rooms. The 'common parlour' had a £20 chimneypiece, and upstairs the price dropped again. The 'one pair of stairs front rooms' had chimneypieces at £10, the back room, clearly of a lower status, had one at only £6. These last were in the price range of the Coade stone or plaster chimneypieces.

Nor was this all, as far as fireplaces are concerned. Under the heading of 'Blacksmith's work', Pain included £67 4s. to pay for the kitchen range, grates, crane (chimney-crane fixed in the chimney to support cauldrons, kettles, etc., above the flames, Plate 70) iron bars to chimneys, iron rails and palisades in front; 36 cwt. of iron at 4½d. per pound. Even allowing for plenty of railings (and I think only street railings are meant, to prevent passers-by falling into the area), this is a startling sum—over £800 in our money. Pain's accounts indicate that between 11% and 12% of the cost of the house went on six chimneypieces, the grates belonging to them, and the kitchen range and its fittings. To give another household cost, for comparison, a 'pretty

70. 18th-century wrought iron chimney-cranes with pot-hangers, from a farmhouse kitchen in Sussex. The crane could be swung in various directions, and the position of the hooks adjusted, so that the contents of a pot on the end of the chain could be cooked at any temperature the cook required.

71. Idleback or kettle-tipper. By pushing on the handle with the knob the kettle could be emptied without unhooking it, or supporting its considerable weight; hence the name idleback, since this device gave a rest to the cook's back muscles. Date uncertain, since its style is traditional; possibly 19th-century.

72. Wrought iron plate-warmer made to stand on the hearth, late 18th-century. The plates were stacked within the ring of uprights, and the upper part could be rotated so that the china warmed evenly. Victoria and Albert Museum.

mahogany four poster bed, with a shaped tester' could be bought from Gillow of Lancaster, in 1793, for £7 14s. Pain's calculations are striking evidence of the importance which the chimneypiece had in the late 18th-century house.

Pain's fireplace equipment consisted of grates. No andirons or firedogs are mentioned. It is time to consider what had been happening inside the fireplace since the end of the 17th century, when, as we have seen, a house such as Ham would have had only one grate and a couple of charcoal-burners to a dozen or more sets of andirons. As coal became the normal fuel, grates became more prevalent, but dating of the designs is difficult for two reasons; first, because the grate or andirons could easily be changed to improve combustion or keep up with the fashions, and second, because contemporary information, in conversation pieces and similar pictures, turns out to be sparse. Artists, rather naturally, were wary of the problems of painting a fireplace with a lighted fire in it, and sometimes the hearth is shown as completely empty. Arthur Devis is a painter who seems to have been interested in household equipment and to have painted it with great accuracy. In a painting in the Walker Art Gallery, Liverpool, he shows a large vase in an otherwise bare fireplace. The vase is empty, but in another painting, at Uppark, Sussex, the fireplace contains a vase full of flowers and this seems to have been the normal place to put a flower arrangement. Josiah Wedgwood consulted a flower decoration expert, so that the shape of his 'bough-pots' should be suitable and convenient for this position.

Another painting by Devis, also at Uppark, shows a fireplace with the fire opening apparently blocked up. This, I think, does not represent anything permanent, but illustrates a chimneyboard, put in place for the summer. The Devis example is absolutely plain, but chimneyboards could be extremely decorative. The designs for two for Osterley Park are still to be seen among the Adam drawings at the Soane Museum, and the actual boards are in their proper places in the house, one in the State Bedroom and one in the Etruscan Room. In both, the scheme of the room and the appropriate colours are repeated on the board. At Heveningham Hall, in Suffolk, the Print Room has its special chimneyboard covered with matching prints. This board has a handle, which must have been a convenience, as the boards were wedged into the fire opening, and must have been difficult to prise out in the autumn. Miss Hamilton, on a visit to the Duchess of Portland in 1783, decorated a chimneyboard in a similar way. 'Mr. Levers, ye house steward, came to me and brought me ye chimney-board he hade made for ye Library, wch I had promised ye Dss [Duchess] to cover wth prints'. She also repaired a chimneyboard ornamented by Mrs Delaney with 'color'd paper, vases, antique figures, &c.', a style of decoration which suggests the Etruscan Room at Osterley. Other chimneyboards were quite plain; Chippendale supplied no less than nine for Nostell Priory, covered with paper, and with a border, for the moderate sum of 4s. each.

While people continued to burn wood as an alternative to coal, andirons were still needed from time to time. There is an interesting grate at Petworth in the Grinling Gibbons Gallery, which may date from the last year or

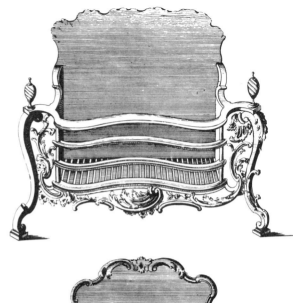

73. Four grates from Thomas Chippendale's *The Gentleman and Cabinet Maker's Director* (1762). Two are rococo, two supposedly Gothick.

two of the 17th century or the beginning of the 18th. It has a firebasket which must have been designed for coal, and also a pair of andirons. These have no back leg, and the billet-bar runs back and forth through loops along the sides of the firebasket. When pushed back and not in use, the *staukes* of the andirons made a decoration at either side of the firebasket. When pulled forward, the andirons could be used to support the logs of a wood fire on the 'down hearth' (the hearthstone itself) in front of the unused coal firebasket.

Andirons were still sufficiently in demand

for Ince and Mayhew to supply designs for them in the grandly titled *Universal System of Household Furniture*, of 1762. These andirons, with a pointed arch and a crocketed finial on the *stauke*, were particularly suited to Gothick chimneypieces, and are shown with them in contemporary designs. Ince and Mayhew also supplied andirons of a nondescript style, which could be used, if necessary, in a rococo or a neoclassical fireplace.

Andirons were by this time generally called dogs, and the combined grate of the Petworth type was known as a dog-grate. It is not possible to tell from the illustrations in the design books at what date the dogs ceased to be moveable, and became merely an extra pair of front legs, attached permanently to the grate. Dog-grates abound in the pattern books from the middle of the century, and Chippendale supplied a number of designs, in all the fashionable styles (Plate 73), in *The Gentleman and Cabinet Maker's Director* (1754). Some of the rococo designs are so elaborate that they must have been extremely difficult to cast. Chippendale was also able to supply both Gothick and Chinese designs, both for grates and chimneypieces, but the most complete fireside equipment in the Chinese style can be found in *A New Book of Chinese Designs* (1754) by Edwards and Darley (Plate 74). They supplied not only a

74. Fireplace suite of grate, bellows, tongs, hearth-brush, shovel, poker and stool (or perhaps trivet) in the chinoiserie taste of the mid-18th century. Plate 65 of *A New Book of Chinese Designs* (1754) by Edwards and Darley.

rather bin-like grate, but also a shovel, tongs and hearth-brush all *en suite*. Faced with the problem of giving the poker a Chinese look, they tormented it into a corkscrew at the point.

Ince and Mayhew made the dog-grate (which they called a stove-grate) neoclassical merely by adding a row of urns along the top. The dog-grate, however, took on its most elegant form in the hands of Adam and his followers. It became wider than before, and stretched across most of the width of the fire opening. The old dogs, now mere rudimentary legs surmounted by urns, were set well outside the firebasket, to which they were joined by sweeping curves of metal. The firebasket itself curved at the base and the curved motif was often continued throughout the whole composition, which might be serpentine, convex or concave. At Osterley, concave dog-grates are set in the concave chimneypieces in the apses of the hall. Robert Adam's elder brother, John, was a partner in the Carron Iron Company, at Falkirk, and it seems probable that these elegant grates (the designs for many of them still among the Adam drawings at the Soane Museum) would have been made by the firm in which the Adams had an interest. Grates were however also made by

75. Bright-cut steel dog-grate in the neoclassical style of Robert Adam, decorated with urns and *paterae*, 1770s. Victoria and Albert Museum.

many other people. One, in the Victoria and Albert Museum, London, (Plate 75) has bright-cut steel ornament, of the type associated with Matthew Boulton in Birmingham. At Corsham ·Court, very handsome steel grates were supplied between 1766 and 1772 by Messrs Alexander and Shrimpton. Here the new fashion of polished steel replaces the traditional marble slips inside the fire opening, and this shining metal, combined with the steel grates, makes the later 18th-century fireplace a much more decorative feature in summer than it had been in the days of plain iron firedogs.

Two wood carvers at the Carron Company, the brothers Howarth, produced admirable designs in the Adam manner for grates, panels, and so on. A favourite design for grates, after the firm obtained a royal charter in 1773, included portrait medallions of George III and Queen Charlotte, elegantly framed in husks and ribbons. The Howarths also designed iron panels with embossed decoration, which were used, as an extension of the old fireback, to line the interior of the fireplace. The fireback itself, shorn of its decorative embossing, and considerably shrunk, was now permanently attached to the dog-grate, where it formed the back of the firebasket.

Many of the Howarth grates were of the hob-grate variety, and it is now time to consider this improvement in grate design. For a long time, some householders had built blocks of brick or masonry on each side of a grate—an example of the 1670s can be seen at Ham House. This helped to keep the grate in position, and provided useful hot surfaces for slow cooking or for keeping food warm. The great advance provided by the hob-grate was to integrate the hobs, now cast in metal, into the grate itself.

The hob-grate stretched right across the fire opening. The grate occupied only about one-third of the space, leaving plenty of hot metal shelving on either side, on which the kettle (which used to hang on a chimney-crane over the fire) came to rest for the next century or so. Sometimes, one or both hobs were designed to open, thus providing oven space inside. Sometimes the hobs were made

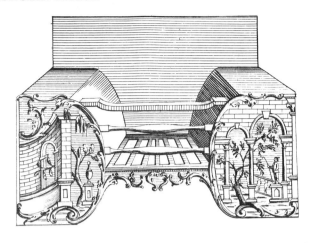

76. Biggin Hall, Northamptonshire. Miniature engraved steel hob-grate of late 18th-century type. It is only about six inches wide, and may have been a traveller's sample.

77. A hob-grate, here called a Bath stove, from Ince and Mayhew's *Universal System of Household Furniture* (1762). The decoration combines classical motifs with chinoiserie.

78. Benjamin Franklin's design for his patent stove, designed to deal with the problem of smoky chimneys. The parts intended to show are neoclassical in style. Figs 1–16 belong to the stove with the urn, figs 18 and 19 show a revolving grate to heat two rooms.

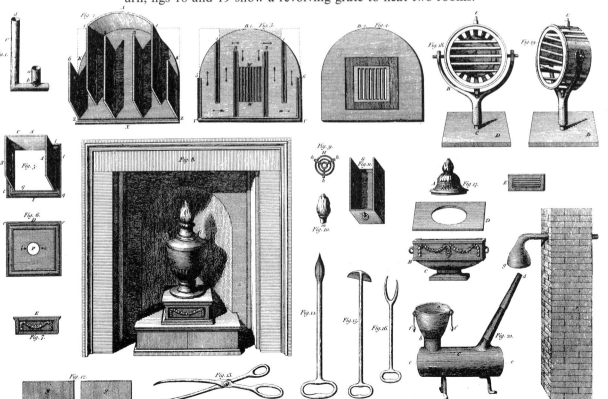

79. Robert Adam's design for a classical stove for the hall of Home House, 20 Portman Square, London. Drawing dated 1776, now in the Soane Museum, London. Stoves of classical design were also used by Adam at Kedleston and at Compton Place, Eastbourne.

separately, and the bars of the firebasket provided the only connection, while at other times the whole front of the grate was treated as one unit, with the firebasket scooped out of it in a semicircle, and a matching semicircle cut out below – a particularly attractive effect (Plate 76).

James Pain's estimate included ironwork for the kitchen range, and it was only a short step from the hob-grate to the cast iron range which, once invented in the late 18th century, has been a kitchen fitment ever since. With much improved insulation and a vitreous enamel finish, its relation can still be bought today. The Howarth type of range, with plenty of enclosed hob space for boiling and frying, must have been a great improvement

on the open fire. Swift had recommended the cook to stir in the smuts which fell into her pan, to add to the flavour – a joke, admittedly, but no doubt the everyday practice of many.

The word 'stove' was in use, but did not always mean the enclosed tiled heating fitment which had been developed in many of the colder countries. Sir Richard Worsley had at Appuldurcombe a stove-grate and no fewer than fifteen Bath stoves (Plate 77). The stove-grate has survived, and is indubitably a hob-grate; the Bath stoves seem likely to have been something of the same kind, since Ince and Mayhew called a hob-grate a Bath stove. They also illustrated what, with a fine disregard for geography, they called a Venetian or Philadelphia stove. This appears to be a grate set in a

80. Burghley House, Northamptonshire. Chimneypiece of porphyry and statuary marble shown in *Diverse Maniere d'Adornari i Cammini* (1769), and described as being 'at Burghley House in England, and made in Rome under the direction and to the design of Cavaliere Gio.Batta. Piranesi.' Piranesi was the artist friend of Robert Adam, Roger Newdigate and other visitors to Rome in the mid-18th century. Early 19th-century grate and fender.

81. *The Lady's Last Stake* (1759) by William Hogarth. It depicts a marble chimneypiece with a contemporary grate ornamented with griffins, a fender across the fire opening, and a *garniture de cheminée* of vases, flowers and a clock. The lady shields her face with a pole firescreen.

large plate of cast iron, designed to fill the whole of the fire opening. Ince and Mayhew say of their specimens that they are 'very useful in preventing smoak'. The real Philadelphia stove (Plate 78) had been invented by Benjamin Franklin, who, like Prince Rupert before him, had interested himself in the problem of smoky chimneys. His design was often pirated in England, and so must have been, to a certain extent, effective. Stoves in our sense were made occasionally. Adam's elegant design of an urn on a tall pedestal, made for Compton Place, is now in the Victoria and Albert Museum, London. He also designed the stoves at Kedleston and Home House (Plate 79) and stoves combined

82. 18th-century fenders in cut steel. As these fenders were put straight across the fire opening (see Hogarth painting, Plate 81) the side return pieces seen in a modern fender were not required. Victoria and Albert Museum.

with pedestals for statues at Newby Hall. James Wyatt designed a classical stove for Dodington House. Apart from these, examples are rare. The Haworths designed what seem, from their drawings, to be stoves of the central European type and called them Chamber stoves, or Canada stoves, but the latter may have been intended for export.

We have seen how, in the 17th century, the fashion for displaying collections of china required a suitable shelf to be put over the fireplace. The Palladian chimneypiece of Inigo Jones usually incorporated such a shelf, as the cornice of the classical entablature always protruded beyond the architrave, and so projected several inches from the wall, thus providing shelf space on its top. When the strictly architectural overmantel, standing on the mantelshelf, was replaced by the painting or mirror hanging on the wall, a whole range of ornaments alighted on the shelf. As symmetrical arrangements seem to have been preferred wherever possible, a *garniture de cheminée* of paired or matching ornaments came into fashion—sets of vases, pairs of candelabra or classical figures, with, perhaps, a clock for a centrepiece. In 1781, Josiah Wedgwood offered a chimneypiece suite of a statue of Mercury, two 'Boys from Fiamingo' and a pair of sphinx candelabra, all in his black basalt ware. Porcelain, bronze and silver were equally appropriate. In his painting *The Lady's Last Stake* (Plate 81), William Hogarth shows a characteristic mantelshelf arrangement. In the middle there is a French clock with a figure of Father Time, and on each side there are small vases of flowers. The candle brackets are attached to the bottom corners of the picture frame above. Hogarth's lady is shielding her face with a firescreen, a useful piece of equipment which had long been known but came into general use at the end of the 17th century (a carved and gilt example designed by John Pelletier is at Hampton Court). The kind used by Hogarth's lady has a tripod stand, and probably has a moveable screen. There was also a type made like a cheval mirror, with the screen swinging between two supports. Sheraton, in his *Cabinet-Maker's and Upholsterer's Drawing Book* (1791–4), calls this a 'Horse Fire Screen'. He could also supply a firescreen of this type fitted with a small drop-down writing desk, and candle brackets at the sides. This pretty but unstable piece of furniture must often have toppled into the fire it was intended to shield. Pole firescreens were not expensive. Gillow, of Lancaster, could supply a charming shield-shaped one for one pound and a farthing, which included 7s. 9d. to Samuel Cooper for making it.

Hogarth's picture shows a painting over the chimneypiece, but mirrors were also fashionable in this position. At Firle Place, Sussex, the two ideas are combined and a portrait is set in an elaborate gilt and mirror frame. A problem, until the 1770s, was the cost of buying a sufficiently large piece of mirror to make a real show. Looking-glass designers were ingenious in evolving imposing openwork frames to camouflage a mosaic of glass pieces. If large plate glasses were essential, they had to be imported from France at enormous expense. To show off the full magnificence of these great sheets of glass, decoration was kept to a narrow border and restrained top cresting. In the course of time, English mirror makers learned the technique of making large plate glass mirrors, and what is thought to be the first English example can be seen in the State Bedroom at Osterley, designed by Robert Adam. Availability made the fashion for these large mirrors more widespread and early in the 19th century a large mirror, usually in a very plain frame, was the normal overmantel decoration.

6. The 19th Century

After the intricate elegance of Adam and his followers had gone out of fashion, simplicity *à la Grecque* became the accepted style. There were no original Greek fireplaces, any more than there were Roman ones, but it seems to have been felt that a very plain chimneypiece, modest in size, would be appropriate to the Greek Doric order at that time most admired. White marble, which had never wholly gone out of fashion, was thought to be Athenian.

The Greek Doric column is not as tall as the Roman column, and this difference in height affected the proportions of both rooms and chimneypieces. Chimneypieces became noticeably lower than those of the late 18th century; both jamb and lintel became narrow, and their decoration severely restrained. There was hardly sufficient depth left to accommodate the central plaque or tablet, and this disappeared from designs. Ornament might consist only of reeding or a simple incised pattern, with perhaps *paterae* or other small ornaments at the corners. Sir John Soane was a master of this austere style (Plates 83, 84), and several of his designs can be seen in his house, which by the terms of his

83. Wimpole Hall, Cambridgeshire. Chimneypiece in the Ante-Library designed by Sir John Soane. An early work (1791), already showing his austere rectangular style. The grate is similar to those in Soane's own house, and is probably contemporary. The mirror and the classical bronze figures holding candelabra are of the Regency period.

84. Port Elliot, Cornwall. Dining-room chimneypiece, 1804–6, designed by Sir John Soane. The spare rectangularity of his design of 1791 (Plate 83) is here carried a stage further. The Greek key-pattern on the jambs is incised. The grate appears to be contemporary.

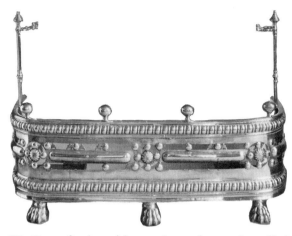

85. Brass fender with cast brass feet and applied rosettes. The fender now curves round at the sides, so that it is free-standing, and has already some of the solidity characteristic of the later 19th century. Formerly in the Macquoid Collection, *c.* 1810.

will became the Soane Museum. A few of Soane's, and his contemporaries', chimney-pieces have a wide projecting mantelshelf, but a characteristic Soanian design is of a kind very common in France, but rare in England. The whole front of the chimneypiece was flat, and set forward nine inches or so from the wall. The top (it can hardly be called a cornice) and the jambs were of the same width. The effect was of a shallow box, set against the wall, with a rectangle cut out for the fire opening. The box-like effect was emphasised by the uncompromising rectangularity of the ornament; variations on the Greek key-pattern incised into the marble were popular.

The grates belonging to these fireplaces shared this same feeling for squareness and simplicity. They were heavier and more solid than 18th-century designs, and the hobs and firebaskets were set lower, and reached barely half-way up the fire opening. (Dog-grates virtually seem to have vanished.) There was much less space below the firebaskets, and this may have been much more practical. 18th-century hob and dog-grates are excellent for radiating heat, but scatter ashes and cinders over a wide area. The fender no doubt moved from its original position, straight across the fire opening, because the ashes fell as often in front of it as behind as soon as the fire was raised up in a high firebasket. Few went to as much trouble to prevent damage by cinders as Queen Charlotte. In 1767, Mrs Lybbe Powis saw in Buckingham House (the Queen's house) 'in every chimney a lacquered wire fireboard, the cleverest contrivance that could be imagined, as even the smallest spark cannot fly through them, while you have heat, and they are really ornamental.' Others were satisfied with half measures, pushing the fender a little further forward. It lay for a time on the part of the hearth within the room, and finally made a border round three sides of this hearth.

A debased classical tradition, which gradually lost sight of the original principles, lingered on into the Victorian period. Chimneypieces became heavier and more clumsy but they remained plain and made of marble, white, or now sometimes brown or salami-coloured. A touch of Soane's incised ornament still adorned the fireplace, and the great sheet of mirror still hung above, now in a narrow gilt or mahogany frame, curved at the top. The arrangement can still occasionally be found in remote station hotels which have not yet been modernised, and children who read *Through the Looking-Glass* in editions with the original Tenniel illustrations will be quite familiar with it. The main difference, when comparing a Regency with a Victorian chimneypiece, lies in the shape of the fire opening. Apart from a few rococo designs, the fire opening had been rectangular since Inigo Jones's day. Now it became an arch. Within it, another arch in cast iron sloped inwards, occupying a large part of the opening, and almost at the base stood the fire-basket. This drastic shrinkage of the fire opening assisted the disposal of smoke, and the large area of metal must have been useful for heat radiation.

Ironfounders, full of enthusiasm in evolving new means of utilising their material, designed iron chimneypieces, which combined the grate and its surround in one metal unit. By the middle of Victoria's reign, astonishingly complicated designs had appeared. The Coalbrookdale catalogue of 1875 shows some feats of casting, if not, perhaps, of design

86–89. Three cast iron fireplaces and a kitchen range from the Coalbrookdale Company's catalogue of 1875.

(Plates 86, 87, 88, 89). One example has caryatids at the sides, putti and shellwork, and a pair of tritons wreathed round the fender. Not so different in theme, perhaps, from Mrs Coade's nautical fireplace, but rather different in effect.

Another unusual material used for fireplaces was pottery. In the first half of the 19th century, a potter called Charles James Mason patented what he called Ironstone China, a wholly misleading title, since his body contained no more stone than any other manufacturer's and no iron at all. Nor was it a china: it was a stoneware. However, it sound-

ed very strong and hard-wearing, and Mason was able to carry out some extraordinary *tours de force* in this material. Among these were some chimneypieces made completely in the ceramic body, which have an engaging rustic, rococo charm (Plate 90). Some were on display in the Great Exhibition of 1851.

Early 19th-century neo-medieval decoration still has some of the confectionary charm of 18th-century Gothick. The 'Perpendicular' chimneypiece designed by Anthony Salvin at Mamhead, Devon, between 1827 and 1833 (Plate 91) bears little relation to a genuine Perpendicular fireplace. It is a gay affair, with very small battlements along the mantelshelf, and a turret-like section at each end enclosing a niche. In the niches are figures of Edward the Confessor and a pilgrim, and the whole composition is painted in red and gold, with blue in the recesses. On either side of the grate are panels painted in pink, blue and gold, and the front of the grate is composed of fleur-de-lys. In spite of Salvin's painstaking collection of medieval motifs, this chimneypiece entirely fails to give any kind of impression of the Middle Ages; the shallow hearth, the tiny fire-basket (useful only for coal) the lacy steel fender – all bring the chimneypiece three centuries forward from its imagined date.

An architect of a rather later date who revelled in an imaginary medieval world was William Burges. At Cardiff he had the remains of a real Gothic castle to re-gothicise and at his home in Kensington he built one of the first suburban houses in the Gothic style, complete with a tower and conical roof. In both places his chimneypieces are spectacular (Plates 92, 93). Burges was a contemporary of

91. Mamhead, Devon. Essay in the Gothic manner by Anthony Salvin, 1827–33. Painted red, gold and blue. The encaustic panels beside the grate are pink, blue and gold and the two little figures are painted in natural colours. The fleurs-de-lys of the grate suggests an early grate at Haddon Hall, but Salvin ran out of inspiration when it came to the fender.

90. Chimneypiece in Mason's patent Ironstone China now at Pigeon Close, Foss Bridge, Gloucestershire. Mason patented his ware (actually an earthenware) in 1813 and made a number of chimneypieces, exhibiting at the Great Exhibition in 1851. The oriental influence in this example suggests a date about 1820, when the Brighton Pavilion had been recently completed. Late 18th-century hob-grate.

the French architect Viollet-le-Duc, at the time working on many ruined châteaux, and many of Burges's ideas are taken from French rather than English models. He loved the great conical fireplace hoods, for instance, and put them in settings supposedly of the English 15th century. The fireplace in the Great Hall at Cardiff Castle illustrates his style at its most exuberant. Painted in natural colours, the fireplace represents the castle itself, with trumpeters on the battlements, ladies waving, a prisoner in a dungeon, and the Duke of Gloucester riding out under the portcullis. Owing to the narrowness of the mantelshelf, he has to ride out sideways. It is all wonderfully gay, and as medieval as Tennyson's *Idylls of the King*.

Few architects seem to have enjoyed themselves quite as much as Burges creating a brilliantly coloured mock Middle Ages, but the impulse towards medievalism remained strong. At Adcote, Shropshire, in 1879, Norman Shaw designed an impressive hooded fireplace of stone, set in a great stone hall with

92. Cardiff Castle, Glamorgan. William Burges's medieval fantasy of 1865, created within the shell of a genuine medieval Great Hall. The fireplace is of Tudor style, with Victorian tiling. The overmantel is supposed to be Cardiff Castle itself, and portrays the Earl of Gloucester riding out to war through the gateway, to a fanfare of trumpets from the castle battlements above. Stone, painted in natural colours.

93. 9 Melbury Road, Kensington, London W.14. One of the many elaborate chimneypieces inspired by medieval fireplaces in the house which William Burges designed for himself between 1875 and 1880. The quadrant-shaped angle brackets, originally designed to hold a rushlight or candle, are here placed immediately under the projecting canopy, so that there is no room to stand a candlestick.

the roof open to the rafters (Plate 94). The firebasket stands almost lost in the cavern of its interior, and there are large and noble firedogs. Inconvenient it may well have been (the fireplace had been getting shallower and smaller for 200 years for purely practical reasons), but visually there is no doubt of its success.

Not content only to create fanciful and often startling interiors, the Victorians felt the need for a more dramatic skyline. The straight cornice and unobtrusive chimneys of the 18th-century houses were thought to be very dull, and turrets, gables and interesting chimneys once more engaged the attention of the architect. Tregothnan, Cornwall, is an early ex-

94. Adcote, Shropshire. 13th-century type of hooded fireplace, designed by Norman Shaw in 1879. Exaggeratedly tall, but impressive hood. The cavernous medieval fireplace is well suggested, though it is neatly lined with tiles and has andirons in the style of the 17th-century.

95. Tregothnan, Cornwall. By William Wilkins, 1816–18, and Lewis Vulliamy, 1845–48. Early 19th-century re-creation of early 16th-century chimneys. The model appears to be East Barsham Manor.

ample to illustrate this (Plate 95). The 17th-century house was altered first by William Wilkins in 1816 and again by Lewis Vulliamy in 1846. They attempted to create an early Tudor manor, and the chimneys will strike a familiar note to the attentive reader, since he will have seen them already. They are based on those at East Barsham Manor, the main difference being that there are even more of them at Tregothnan. From this time on, the skylines of 19th-century houses were spiked with an endless palisade of fancy chimneys, often picturesque and occasionally efficient.

To improve this efficiency, there were all kinds of devices, the most noticeable being the chimneypot. Though they had long been in existence, it was during the 19th-century that they reached the peak of their dreadful variety. Doré's illustrations of London make this appallingly clear; and they also make clear, in the plumes of smoke shown puffing out of all of them, the inefficiency of the fireplaces below. The Victorian householder noticed the disarray of his chimneypots no more than the modern householder notices the assorted ironmongery of television aerials he has instead. The purpose of the chimneypots was utilitarian. His aim was not to get rid of smoke through better combustion, an ideal beyond him, but quite simply to get smoke up the chimney instead of into the rooms.

Early chimneys were very wide; it is still often possible to stand on an old farmhouse hearth and see a good patch of sky at the top of the chimney. As coal became the more usual fuel, and the smoke entering the room more acrid, chimney flues were narrowed in an attempt to persuade the smoke more effectively up the chimney. At times they were as narrow as a foot or nine inches, and this meant not only that the soot was deposited over a smaller area than before, and was therefore thicker, but also that it was much more difficult to get at. Extreme measures such as throwing burning hay down the chimney, or deliberately allowing it to catch fire from the bottom, often set the whole house on fire as well; and in the early years of the 18th century the appalling habit developed of sending small children up the chimneys to sweep out the soot (Plate 96). Sometimes they stuck, and a line or two in a news sheet would mention their end, among other interesting disasters; mostly, they got down, black and rubbed raw, to climb again until mercifully they grew too big even to squeeze into the bottom of the chimney. Among the other miseries of child labour in the 18th and 19th centuries, the plight of the chimneysweeps did not seem to call for any special concern. A few people were kind; Mrs Montagu gave the little sweeps a feast every May Day; Lamb's essay on the sweep suggests that 'It is good to give him a penny; it is better to give him twopence', but the only result of Jonas Hanway's bill in Parliament, in 1788, was to restrict the apprenticeship of sweeps to those aged eight and over. It took a royal commission, and Kingsley's picture, in the *Water Babies*, of Grimes and his wretched child assistant, to push through Parliament an act finally abolishing child sweeps in 1875, after 150 years of exploitation. Only very occasionally did a child sweep have the luck of young Isaac Ware, who was seen making a chalk drawing of the Banqueting House in Whitehall on the stone of the building itself. The gentleman who observed him got him from his master without difficulty, as he was puny and feeble, had him educated in England and Italy, and eventually had the pleasure of

96. Child sweep of the mid-19th century.

97. The Red House, Bexley, Kent. Fireplace in the house designed for William Morris by Philip Webb in 1859. The shape of the fireplace, in brick, recalls the medieval canopy over the hearth. The interior of the fireplace has been modernised. The fireplaces in this house, of natural brickwork, anticipate by half a century the thousands of brick fireplaces built between 1910 and 1930.

seeing him develop into the distinguished Palladian architect whose lively views on chimneypieces have been quoted in this book.

Elizabethan and Jacobean architecture, with its rich profusion of Renaissance and medieval motifs, had an exuberance which appealed to many Victorians. Many were the new versions of Burghley House or Wollaton, Hatfield or Hardwick Hall, all complete with neo-Elizabethan chimneypieces. We have seen them on their first appearance, and there is no need to linger over them as they come round again. An artist who re-interpreted the past in a different way was William Morris. In his backward look beyond the Industrial Revolution to a world in which the self-sufficient craftsman carried through all aspects of his work himself, Morris hoped to find inspiration in the simpler 16th and 17th-century houses, and the furniture made by the village carpenter from local materials. In 1859, he commissioned young Philip Webb to design a house in the country–the Red House–which had a profound effect on domestic design. A fireplace in this house illustrates the ideas of Webb and Morris. Here, both the fire opening and the chimneybreast above it are made of plain red brick, partly laid in a herring-bone pattern. At the top, about eight feet up, the thickness of the brick forms a narrow shelf to hold the blue and white plates which were again returning to fashion. In another, upstairs, both hearth and medieval hooded chimney are made of brick (Plate 97).

The Red House is now part of the London suburbs and its decoration has ceased to be unique. All over Britain there are hundreds and thousands of houses with fireplaces made of bare brick, with old oak lintels, farmhouse inglenooks and wrought iron firebaskets, all of them stemming from the Red House and built during the last century. Morris's influence turned the taste of his day away from the sophisticated design of the past, and convinced professional and upper class Englishmen (except the *very* rich, who stuck to the 'style Rothschild', as at Waddesdon Manor) that their ideal home was the cottage or farmhouse in the country which had previously been inhabited exclusively by the farmer, the smith or the sexton. From the seventies and eighties, architects were asked to produce houses which were cottages in style, though they were mansions in size. Genuine cottages were adapted, and old cavernous fireplaces, with their blackened chimneybeams, were excavated once more from the plasterwork which had enclosed them in the 17th and 18th centuries. Open fires, of logs if possible, became popular again, and the local smith was set to hammer out andirons and firebaskets once more. The farmhouse style had an extraordinarily long run. As late as the 1920s and even the 1930s, cottage-style fireplaces in ancient bricks were being built in cottage-style houses around London.

Victorian design lacked a universally accepted standard of 'correct taste', such as had guided Georgian architects. By the last quarter of the century, medieval buildings were not the only models, and W. S. Gilbert, in the operetta *Patience* (1881) was able to ridicule those aesthetes to whom the 'age of good Queen Anne was culture's palmiest day'. This neo-Queen-Anne was an eclectic style. A house in Queen's Gate, Kensington, designed by Norman Shaw only four years after his pastiche of the 13th century at Adcote, has a drawing-room with an Adam ceiling, windows with mullions and transoms of remotely Jacobean origin, and a chimneypiece which is rather old-fashioned for Queen Anne's reign, though it could well have been designed in her lifetime (Plate 98); it relates to the chimney-pieces at such houses as Belton or Groom-bridge Place. It is an agreeable re-creation of a period in which chimneypieces were going through one of their more modest phases.

The general run of architects, even by the end of the century, had not got this far. Few ordinary houses had chimneypieces as simple and sensible as those at 180 Queen's Gate. In the average house (excluding those influenced by the Morris Arts and Crafts movement) the chimneypiece itself was reasonably plain, but was surmounted by a very complicated overmantel. Usually this was of wood, stained or painted, with a mass of small fretwork shelves on which the housewife could arrange her collection of figurines and vases. There would be at least one, and often many, inset pieces of looking-glass, and sometimes the whole construction would be backed with mirror. A fairly restrained example, in Mrs Panton's book for brides *From Kitchen to Garret* (1887), shows separate brackets for seven vases and a fair-sized clock. It had been customary, since the middle of the century, to drape a pelmet along the mantelshelf. Mrs Panton recommended a goffered frill of cretonne, or a Bokhara plush. She put Japanese fans as a background to photographs, a clock, spill-vases, some copper candlesticks, and 'one of the tall sixpenny Liberty vases' with a single rose or two; while for summer use, she hid the grate with a Japanese parasol. She recommended that the overmantel and board be painted sage-green, 'if possible with sprays of pale pink roses or chrysanthemums on'. In the dining-room, the grate in summer was to become a conservatory, with a fender of virgin cork, covered with moss and inset with jam jars in which flowers were arranged. A handbasin in the grate was to hold peonies, but Mrs Panton warned her readers that only the aspidistra could be expected to flourish in this position.

It was not surprising that equipment for tending the fire became more elaborate; shovels, tongs, hearth-brushes and pokers were made *en suite*. They could be hung together on a stand placed on the hearth, and often had brass or copper decoration. It was still thought rather unsuitable for the coal to be kept in the room (Mrs Panton made it clear that a coal-scuttle was a modernism to

98. 180 Queen's Gate, London S.W.7. Norman Shaw's 'Queen Anne', 1883. A handsome bolection-moulded chimneypiece in two shades of marble, possibly based on a design with a similar dark strip of marble at Belton House, Lincolnshire. The fender is ingeniously made from a further section of bolection moulding, laid flat.

be accepted with reservations) but it was now held in a brass or copper container. This was sometimes shaped, after a fashion, like a classical helmet. Auctioneers' catalogues elegantly called it a 'purdonium', but it remained a coal-scuttle none the less. Fenders were sometimes elaborate, and a curious tall species, with a padded top which formed a small seat, was known as a 'Club Fender'. It ruined the proportions of the chimneypiece, but was a

comfort, not so much for the men, who are always shown in Victorian drawings as standing in front of the fire, with their coat tails lifted to get the benefit of the heat, but for the ladies of the family–who may, however, at times have singed their bustles.

The *fin de siècle* fashions belong as much to the beginning of the 20th century as to the end of the 19th, and they will be dealt with in the next chapter.

7. The 20th Century

The homespun style which William Morris originated was as popular after 1900 as before it – indeed more so, if we compare the number of pseudo-farmhouses built in the 1890s with the thousands of 'dream' cottages, complete with brick hearths, built in the 1920s. Art Nouveau is another style which spanned the turn of the century. Gas and electricity for heating and cooking – fuels which, with oil, are now bringing the history of the English fireplace to a close – were already well known before 1900, but had their full impact afterwards.

Art Nouveau, the style which has no English name, but which the Italians call the Liberty style after the London shop, had different origins from the Morris craft movement. Now that it has become fashionable once again, we get more than enough of the flamboyant, boneless forms which characterise the decorative elements of Art Nouveau, and are apt to forget that, in the British Isles, at least, Art Nouveau architecture owed much to the bold austerities of Victorian engineering. In the hands of one of the pioneers, Charles Rennie Mackintosh, Art Nouveau had a spare cold elegance which heralded the architecture of the mid-20th century (Plate 101). The rubbery stems and sinuous lines which we associate with Art

99. Standen, East Grinstead, Sussex. Designed by Philip Webb, 1891–94. Cottagey inspiration in the large brick-lined fire opening, combined with details influenced by Voysey in the high, boldly projecting mantelshelf, the simple mouldings and the shiny white paint. Logs made the fire once more, and ancient andirons were brought back into use, or copied by the local blacksmith.

100. Tigbourne Court, Surrey. Chimneys of 17th-century style designed by Sir Edwin Lutyens in 1899.

101. Fireplace designed by Charles Rennie Mackintosh, *c.* 1904, for the Willow Tea-rooms, Glasgow. Victoria and Albert Museum.

Nouveau were used as decoration, but underneath there was a plain and logical structure. However, the proportions of some features are curious: a very large chimneypiece could have a minute fire opening, while mantelpieces ceased to be shelves on which an elbow could be comfortably supported, and shot up towards the ceiling. Still, there was a welcome clearance of the Victorian fretwork. Paint was white and shiny, edges were squared-off rather than moulded, and decoration was sparse. These characteristics can be found even in the work of architects deeply influenced by the theories of William Morris. Voysey, Gimson and Barnsley designed country houses which in their gables and picturesquely clustered chimneys looked back to the Jacobean Cotswold tradition (Plate 100), but whose mullioned casements opened into trim white interiors. Tiles were often used with success—the blue and white Dutch, and the blue and green designs by

102. Gas fire made by Wilson's as early as 1877. Its shape resembles a teacosy.

103), or shaped into a quadrant form and laid in the hearth. These latter were extraordinarily long-lasting; gas fires of this type installed in late Edwardian times could still be used in the 1950s, though they were inefficient by modern standards. Gas fires had to be set in a fireplace but there was little of the up-draught of a coal or wood fire and there were regularly voiced complaints that gas fires dried the atmosphere. For decades, a pie-dish, full of water, had to be laid on the hearth, in the hope that the evaporation of the water would get the atmosphere back to normal. Gas stoves made cooking a great deal less troublesome, but the new invention was not welcomed for some time. Cooks accustomed to the mystique

William de Morgan, based on Persian or Isnik originals, were particularly popular. Halsey Ricardo, de Morgan's partner, notable for the astonishing polychrome-tiled house he built in Addison Road, London, designed himself a most effective drawing-room with a white chimneypiece and a chimneybreast almost completely covered with de Morgan tiles in a Persian design.

Chimneypieces were still large in the entertaining rooms, and the hall (which was now apt to be a large draughty room intended to recall the medieval Great Hall) often had a version of the farmhouse open fireplace, with exposed beams and brass or copper kitchen utensils. In the smaller rooms, however, the chimneypiece shrank to the neat sizes of the late 17th century and was often fitted, in 17th-century style, across a corner. This shrinkage could conveniently take place, following the invention of the gas fire. Gas lighting was known from the early 19th century, though not generally used until later. (Mrs Panton thought it unbecoming, though she was of course fighting a losing battle.) Gas heating was introduced later, but was well in use by the 1880s. A very early gas fire, of the seventies, has an ingenious shape like a teacosy (Plate 102). Later, the elements for the fires were made of a white ceramic substance in a vermiculated pattern. Panels of it could be stood upright in metal cabinets (some with doors and Art Nouveau decoration, Plate

103. 'Melrose' gas fire (R. and A. Main Ltd.) of the Edwardian period. The side wings, with glass panels, could be closed when the fire was not in use, and the flat area on the top could be used for cooking.

of the correctly stoked coal range fought a rear-guard action against the much more manageable gas cooker. When, as late as the 1920s, Queen Mary was presented with the Queen's Doll's House, an exact miniature of the ideal house of the time, the kitchens were still fitted with tiny coal ranges. Gas was considered to produce an insidious 'back-taste' detectable by fastidious palates, since the smell of uncombusted gas was imagined into dishes cooked by the odourless and tasteless combusted gas. When the coal range was removed from the fireplace which it had occupied since the late 18th century, the recess was often tiled, and the gas cooker stood in the recess. It was a long time before it was realised that the cooker could be released from the fireplace, and stand in any convenient position.

104. 'Apollo' electric fire, *c*. 1904. Cast metal. Heating elements in glass 'envelopes'.

Electric lighting was known, as a luxury feature of the house, towards the end of the last century, but was rare in town, and rarer still in the country, where it was sometimes generated on large estates. Until the grid system was completed, electric fires and cooking were only for the town-dweller. Again, the development was the same as with gas, with the cooker and the fire only very gradually separating themselves from the fireplace. During the inter-war period, for instance, when electric fires had become normal in bedrooms, it was still usual to build houses with fireplace surrounds filled in with something like the 18th-century chimneyboard. The electric fire was set into the middle of this. Such an arrangement, of course, was normal in old houses, where a fireplace existed already. Even when the house had central heating, quite elaborate chimneypieces were still supplied for the main entertaining rooms, and most houses had at least one fireplace where a coal or log fire was lit throughout the winter. Central heating, in any case, was until after the last war normally put only in the sitting-rooms and the hall or passages. Bedrooms were left cold, except for the *ad hoc* gas or electric fires, as it was assumed that they would get sufficient background heat filtering in from the radiators in the hall.

We have seen ceramic plaques inset into chimneypieces in the 18th century, and Mason's completely ceramic chimneypieces of the 19th century. During the inter-war period, ceramic chimneypieces returned to fashion. Tiles had, of course, long been used on the inside of the fireplace, first inside the fire opening, and then, as the opening gradually got smaller, as a decoration on the front, and on the hearth. As householders tired of the positive (and immovable) colours of Victorian tiles—dark red, iridescent green, or perhaps Dutch blue and white—builders supplied fireplaces tiled in colours to match beige, the decoration colour of those decades. All shades of cream, oatmeal, buff, mud and stone were available, either plain or mottled. The tile manufacturers provided their own surrounds to replace the older wooden ones, so that the whole chimneypiece could be in tile. A typical design had the mantelshelf

105. Another form of firedog. This fireplace was shown in *Black Eyes and Lemonade*, a 'pop art' exhibition before its time held at the Whitechapel Art Gallery in the early 1950s. The fireplace seems to have been a design in regular production at that time.

106. Fireplace installed in a hotel in Wimbledon in the early 1950s. A manifestation of the nostalgia which produced, about the same time, a half-timbered buffet car for British Railways.

107. 'Haddon Hall' fireplace by Minsterstone Ltd. A very popular type of fireplace during the inter-war period. Based on a Tudor fireplace, but, unlike the original, projecting from the chimneybreast, and with a raised hearth incorporating the fender. The grate includes andirons and seems to be based on a very early grate at Plas Mawr, Wales.

108. Inter-war period gas fire with imitation coals and a further archaism in the steel firedogs. With a coal fire, firedogs still sometimes had a vestigial use as props for the poker, shovel and hearth-brush. Possibly the designer of this imitation coal fire intended it to be accompanied by a ritual poker and tongs on the hearth, to add realism.

raised in the centre and various cubist-patterned tiles, in orange and brown, inset here and there. Sometimes a small chimney-piece would be fired in one piece, with lines incised on it to represent the divisions of the tiles. Possibly the nastiest was a post-war design for a child's room, and represented an airedale dog (Plate 105). Other ceramic fire-places were made of a stone-like body. These were made of large blocks, the equivalent size of dressed blocks of stone, and were usually of Tudor design (Plate 107). Mouldings, the flattened arch of the fire opening, and the

Tudor roses set in the corners, followed 16th-century precedent; but the genuine fireplace of Henry VIII's time was set flush with the wall, whereas its 20th-century imitation projected seven or eight inches, to allow enough space on the top to make a mantelshelf. The hearth, too, was raised, and shaped in one piece with its fender, in the modern version. However, it went well enough into the neo-Elizabethan houses still being built in the reign of George VI. Ceramic chimneypieces, in more modern designs, are in active production today.

When the coal fire was still the natural alternative to a gas or electric fire, it was not surprising that these new fuels should take on camouflage, so that their more traditional appearance might attract the more conservative buyer. Imitation coal and log fires (Plate 108), available from 1921 in imitation dog-grates, were very popular. A hood turning round an electric light bulb produced a flickering light in the glowing pseudo-coal, while an electric element provided the real heating. This element could be turned off separately, leaving a cold and particularly cheerless travesty of a genuine fire. Such objects seem to belong to an age when gas and electric heating were not acceptable in their own right, and it would have seemed likely that they would have disappeared long since. Not at all; if we are to believe the advertisements, they are more popular now than they were a decade ago, and they can now be supplied with lighting which imitates the random variations of natural flames instead of the repetitive pattern of the older lamp.

All this imitation seems a pity, when heaters of all types, gas, electric and oil, are moving away from radiant to convected heat, with the consequent concealment of the source of heat. This has meant that at last the heating unit can safely emancipate itself from the fireplace, without any risk of the furniture being set alight by a heating element placed too close. With the parallel development of central heating, the home should in time become a less dangerous place than statistics tell us that it is.

When L. A. Shuffrey wrote his book *The English Fireplace* in 1912, every room had its

109. A modern interpretation of the medieval hooded fireplace. By Ted Levy and Associates in a house in Hampstead, London.

110. Another interpretation of the medieval conception of the central hearth. Here the fireplace is between living areas and heats both. The hearth is raised to provide heat at a convenient level for people seated by the fire. Architects: Chamberlin, Powell, and Bon.

fireplace, and at times its coal fire; as late as the twenties, even offices still had them. The last fifty-six years have seen an almost complete change, and all public places are now warmed to the even temperature produced by central heating. The modern open-plan house, with its huge windows, would be unspeakably draughty without radiators or warm convected air. Max Beerbohm had a theory that English women's complexions had their particular bloom because they were perpetually being surprised by changes of temperature, from a roasting fire to near freezing corridors. If he is right the bland level temperatures of today may be one reason why beauty preparations have such an excellent sale.

Even in our agreeable, centrally heated micro-climate, when we ought to be able to do without them, fireplaces and fires still seem to fill some ancestral need. It should be possible by now to write the last chapter in the history of the English fireplace, but clearly it is not. Even if it is only a showpiece, most houses still retain one fireplace, and good and imaginative designs have been evolved in recent years (Plates 109, 110, 111), some of them going back to the old Anglo-Saxon idea of the central hearth. In the United States, reconstituted logs made of sawdust, and of convenient standard size, are available for fireplaces, which are a status symbol adding greatly to the value of a house. A focus, we learn from the dictionary, comes from the Latin word for the hearth; and it seems to be taking us a very long time to dispense, finally, with the focal point of our homes.

111. A fireplace with some of the qualities of a stove but with the fire itself open to the room. The fire, burning wood, is again raised to a comfortable height. Fireplace by Wren Fireplaces Ltd.

Buildings open to the Public

The buildings listed below, and mentioned in this book, are open to the public. The list is correct at the time of going to press, but access to some of them is restricted, and readers should consult the current guide book before planning a visit.

Arbury Hall, Warwickshire
Belton House, Lincolnshire
Bisham Abbey, Berkshire
Boynton Hall, Yorkshire
Burghley House, Northamptonshire
Burton Agnes Hall, Yorkshire
Cardiff Castle, Glamorgan
Castle Hedingham, Essex
Castle Howard, Yorkshire
Charlton House, Greenwich, London
Chatsworth, Derbyshire
Chiswick House, Middlesex
Clandon Park, Surrey
Claydon House, Buckinghamshire
Cobham Hall, Kent
Colchester Castle, Essex
Corsham Court, Wiltshire
East Barsham Manor, Norfolk
Farnborough Hall, Warwickshire
Gainsborough Old Hall, Lincolnshire
Gilling Castle, Yorkshire
Glastonbury Abbey, Somerset
Ham House, Surrey
Hampton Court Palace, Middlesex
Hardwick Hall, Derbyshire

Hatfield House, Hertfordshire
Heveningham Hall, Suffolk
Lanhydrock, Cornwall
Longleat, Wiltshire
Loseley House, Surrey
Mawley Hall, Worcestershire
Michelham Priory, Sussex
Montacute, Somerset
Muchelney Abbey, Somerset
Newby Hall, Yorkshire
Osterley Park, Middlesex
Penshurst Place, Kent
Petworth House, Sussex
The Queen's House, Greenwich, London
Rochester Castle, Kent
Rufford Old Hall, Lancashire
Sawston Hall, Cambridgeshire
The Soane Museum, London
Sydenham House, Devonshire
Syon House, Middlesex
Tattershall Castle, Lincolnshire
Uppark, Sussex
Wilton House, Wiltshire
Woburn Abbey, Bedfordshire
Wollaton Hall, Nottinghamshire

Index

Plate numbers are indicated in bold type.